ENGLISCH IM BERUF

WORTSCHATZ WIRTSCHAFTS-ENGLISCH

Gisela Groß

Wortschatz Wirtschaftsenglisch
Ein Arbeits- und Übungsbuch

Verfasserin: Gisela Groß

Verlagsredaktion: Helga Holtkamp

Herstellung: Sabine Trittin

1. Auflage

5.	4.	3.	2.	1.	Die letzten Ziffern bezeichnen Zahl und
96	95	94	93	92	Jahr des Druckes

Alle Drucke dieser Auflage können, weil untereinander unverändert, im Unterricht nebeneinander verwendet werden.

Bestellnummer: 24679

© Cornelsen & Oxford University Press GmbH, Berlin

Das Werk und seine Teile sind urheberrechtlich geschützt. Jede Verwertung in anderen als den gesetzlich zugelassenen Fällen bedarf deshalb der vorherigen schriftlichen Einwilligung des Verlages.

Druck: Saladruck
Weiterverarbeitung: Hensch

ISBN 3-8109-2467-9

Vertrieb: Cornelsen Verlagsgesellschaft, Bielefeld

Inhaltsverzeichnis

Vorwort	4
1. Verschiedene Übersetzungsmöglichkeiten deutscher Begriffe ins Englische	7
Übungen zu Kapitel 1	30
2. Englische Wörter mit Doppel- und Mehrfachbedeutungen	34
Übungen zu Kapitel 2	47
3. Der richtige Umgang mit Fremdwörtern	49
Übungen zu Kapitel 3	56
4. Wortgruppen	57
Übungen zu Kapitel 4	83
5. Vorsicht: Fallen und Sünden	84
Übungen zu Kapitel 5	98
6. Vorsicht auch bei der Orthographie	99
Übungen zu Kapitel 6	101
7. Abkürzungen	103
8. Präpositionen	109
Übungen zu Kapitel 8	122
9. Britisches und amerikanisches Englisch	124
10. Schlüssel zu den Übungen	129

Vorwort

Während meiner langjährigen Tätigkeit als Leiterin der Übersetzungsabteilung eines bedeutenden Industrieunternehmens und als Dozentin, die angehende Fremdsprachenkorrespondenten für die Prüfung vor der Industrie- und Handelskammer ausbildet, ist mir eins immer wieder bewußt geworden: die Arbeit mit einer Fremdsprache wird vielfach einfach zu leicht genommen und deshalb werden oft Fehler gemacht, die man vermeiden könnte. Schlimmstenfalls sind es grobe Übersetzungsfehler oder Sinnfehler. Aber auch sprachliche Ungenauigkeiten und nicht treffende Formulierungen können zeitraubende Rückfragen verursachen und die Kommunikation empfindlich stören.
Die häufig herrschende Meinung, Englisch sei eine leicht zu erlernende Sprache, ist nur bedingt richtig. Zugegeben, wenn man an die Anfänge denkt, so kann man diese Ansicht durchaus vertreten. Wie viele Formen eines Verbs muß man beispielsweise im Deutschen, im Französischen oder im Spanischen lernen, bis man einfache Sätze richtig formulieren kann. Da hat man es im Englischen wirklich leichter. Sie, als in der Wirtschaft oder in Handel und Industrie Tätige(r), sollten aber möglichst ein Sprachniveau haben, bei dem die Aussage, Englisch sei leicht, längst nicht mehr zutrifft.
Ich habe deshalb die von Kolleginnen und Kollegen sowie von Kursteilnehmern und -teilnehmerinnen oft gemachten kleinen und großen Fehler gesammelt, und das war der Anfang des vorliegenden Buches. Es verging kein Tag, an dem mir nicht irgend jemand Stoff für die einzelnen Kapitel lieferte und meine Meinung bestätigte, daß viel zu viele Fehler gemacht werden – teils aus Unwissenheit, teils aber auch nur aus Gedankenlosigkeit. Leider wissen viele Leute in der Praxis gar nicht, daß und wie fehlerhaft ihre Übersetzungen und Mitteilungen an Kunden sind.
Nehmen Sie die Texte, die Sie zu bearbeiten haben, ernst, verwenden Sie also die größte Sorgfalt darauf, daß in der Zielsprache auch wirklich zum Ausdruck kommt, was in der Ausgangssprache gesagt wird. Oft sind Übersetzungen in die Muttersprache schlechter oder ungenauer als solche in die Fremdsprache. Das liegt mit Sicherheit daran, daß man nicht mit genügender Aufmerksamkeit an die Übersetzung geht, denn „Deutsch kann ich ja". Der deutsche Text mag sich dabei sogar recht gut anhören, nur sagt er nicht das aus, was im fremdsprachlichen Text steht. Die Tatsache, daß die englische Sprache der deutschen häufig recht ähnlich ist, kann gefährlich werden, wenn man die feinen Bedeutungsunterschiede nicht beachtet.
Die Einteilung des Buches in verschiedene Kapitel wurde nach unterschiedlichen Gesichtspunkten gemacht. Sie dient in erster Linie dem Zweck, auf Besonderheiten hinzuweisen und so mögliche Fehler von vornherein auszuschalten. Sieben der insgesamt neun Kapitel haben am Ende einen Übungsteil. Der Lösungsschlüssel befindet sich am Ende des Buches.

Wortschatz Wirtschaftsenglisch richtet sich an verschiedene Zielgruppen: zum einen an diejenigen, die ein zusätzliches Lehr- und Übungsbuch für die Aus- und Weiterbildung suchen, zum anderen an die, die sich im Selbststudium weiterbilden wollen, und – last but not least – an die vielen „Praktiker", die beruflich mit Wirtschaftsenglisch zu tun haben. Gerade im Hinblick auf ein vereintes Europa wird diese Gruppe immer größer, und Fremdsprachen – besonders Englisch – werden immer wichtiger.

Benutzer(innen), die noch in der Ausbildung stehen, sollten die Kapitel zunächst gründlich durcharbeiten, anschließend die dazugehörigen Übungen machen und dann das Ergebnis mit dem Schlüssel vergleichen. In manchen Fällen gibt es natürlich mehr als eine richtige Übersetzung oder Lösung, aus Platzgründen habe ich aber immer nur eine korrekte Variante angegeben. Bei der Wahl der Beispielsätze und Übungen wurden weitgehend Begriffe der Korrespondenz- und Wirtschaftssprache verwendet.

Die Berufstätigen haben ein Nachschlagewerk, das ihnen bei der täglichen Arbeit so manchen nützlichen Hinweis gibt, und sie können gleichzeitig etwas für die Vervollkommnung ihrer Englischkenntnisse tun. Sie schauen nicht nur einen gerade fehlenden Begriff nach, sondern erinnern sich, „daß da doch noch etwas zu beachten ist", und lesen kurz nach, um was es sich handelt. Natürlich erhebt das Buch keinen Anspruch auf Vollständigkeit, aber es sicherlich geeignet, die Benutzer(innen) zu sensibilisieren, vorsichtig mit der Fremdsprache umzugehen. Ich hoffe, daß ich mit **Wortschatz Wirtschaftsenglisch** sowohl den noch in der Ausbildung Befindlichen, als auch den bereits Berufstätigen eine Hilfe für ihre Arbeit an die Hand geben konnte.

Gisela Groß

1. Verschiedene Übersetzungsmöglichkeiten deutscher Begriffe ins Englische

Dieses Verzeichnis zeigt auf, wie viele Bedeutungen ein deutsches Wort haben kann, und soll Ihnen helfen, den jeweils richtigen englischen Begriff zu finden, um adäquat zu übersetzen.
Nur große Wörterbücher sind in der Lage, die Unterschiede richtig herauszustellen. Bei ihrer Verwendung benötigt man oft viel Zeit, um das richtige Wort in der richtigen Wendung zu finden.
Von Anfängern im Sprachunterricht kommt häufig die Frage, welches Wörterbuch sie sich kaufen sollen, und viele sind erstaunt, wenn vor der Verwendung eines Wörterbuchs zunächst einmal gewarnt wird, „bis der Zeitpunkt gekommen ist, daß Sie damit umgehen können".
Eigentlich sollte man ein Wort hauptsächlich dann in einem Wörterbuch nachsehen, wenn man es irgendwann einmal gelernt hat, es einem aber im Moment entfallen ist. Sieht man es dann wieder, erinnert man sich und weiß, ob es paßt. Es kann außerordentlich gefährlich sein, irgendein Wort einzusetzen, das man nicht kennt. Es kann passieren, daß das, was man sagen will, überhaupt nicht oder sehr ungenau ausgedrückt wird.
Läßt es sich aber einmal nicht vermeiden, daß Sie ein Wort nachschlagen, so sollten Sie in jedem Falle die Gegenprobe machen, d.h. das gefundene Wort im jeweils anderssprachigen Wörterbuchteil nachsehen. Es kann vorkommen, daß Sie es dort nicht finden, und zwar dann, wenn ein solches Wort nur in einen ganz bestimmten Kontext paßt.
Es ist zwar richtig, daß viele Ausländer es schätzen, wenn man überhaupt in ihrer Sprache mit ihnen korrespondiert, aber wenn das dann noch in gutem, unmißverständlichen Englisch geschieht, wird es Ihre Ausgangsposition mit Sicherheit verbessern.
Nachfolgend deshalb ein *word study* einmal auf eine etwas andere Art als allgemein üblich:

a

Ablauf
(Abfluß) *outlet*
(von Ereignissen) *course*
(von Flüssigkeiten) *drainage*
Ablauf eines Vertrages *expiry of a contract*
nach Ablauf des Jahres *at the end of the year*
bei Ablauf von *on expiration of*
Ablauffrist *expiry date*

Abnahme
(Annahme) *acceptance*
(Prüfung) *quality control/inspection*
(Verringerung) *decrease*
(von Interesse, Nachfrage) *decline*
die Abnahme verweigern *to refuse acceptance, to reject*
Abnahmebeamter *quality controller/ inspector*

Abnahmemöglichkeit *acceptability*
Abnahmetest *acceptance test*

Absatz
(Abschnitt) *paragraph*
(von Schuh) *heel*
(Ablagerung) *deposit*
(Verkauf) *sales*
Absatzchance *sales potential*
absatzfähig *marketable, saleable*
Absatzmarkt *market*
Absatzschwierigkeiten *sales problems*

abziehen
(entfernen) *to remove, to take off, to strip off*
(Fell, Haut) *to skin, to flay*
(Kapital, Truppen) *to withdraw*
(Schlüssel) *to take out*

(mathematisch)	to substract	**Ansicht**	
(schleifen)	to grind, to resharpen	(Meinung)	opinion, view
(vervielfältigen)	to xerox, to copy	(Betrachten, Prüfen)	inspection
(losschießen)	to discharge	(Veranschaulichung	
(weggehen)	to depart, to go away, to leave	eines Teils)	view
		Ansicht im Aufriß	elevation
		kritische Ansicht	criticism
Abzug	removal, withdrawal, departure	zur Ansicht	for your inspection
		Waren zur Ansicht schicken	to send goods on approval
(von Lohn)	deduction	**Ansichtskarte**	picture postcard
(Rabatt)	discount	**Außenansicht**	exterior
(am Gewehr)	trigger	**Innenansicht**	interior
(von Foto)	print		
Korrekturabzug	proof	**Antwort**	answer, response, reaction, reply
ändern	to alter	**antworten**	to answer
(hinzufügen)	to amend	(reagieren)	to react/respond (to)
(dabei verbessern)	to modify	auf einen Brief antworten	to reply to a letter, to answer a letter
(wechseln)	to change		
sich ändern	to change	**Beantwortung**	reply
geänderte Rechnung	amended invoice	in Beantwortung Ihres Briefes vom 16. Januar	in reply to your letter of 16th January
Änderung	alteration, amendment, modification, change		
anfangen	to start, to begin, to commence	**Arbeit**	
		(Tätigkeit)	work
(in die Wege leiten)	to initiate	(mehr körperlich)	labour
		(Mühe)	trouble
Anlage		(Abhandlung)	treatise
(Fabrik)	facility	(von Gerät, System)	function
(Geld)	investment	(Aufgabe)	task, job
(Maschine)	plant	**Arbeitsamt**	employment exchange, [GB] job centre
(zu Schriftstück)	enclosure		
(Begabung)	talent	**Arbeitskampf**	industrial action
		Arbeitsmarkt	labour market
Annahme		**Arbeitsstelle**	job, place of work
(Entgegennahme)	acceptance	**Arbeitsweise**	
(Vermutung)	assumption, supposition	(von Maschinen)	method/mode of operation
(Hypothese)	hypothesis		
(Zustimmung)	acceptance	(von Menschen)	working practice
(eines Kindes)	adoption	**Arbeitszeit**	working hours
bedingte Annahme	qualified acceptance	**arbeiten**	to work
die Annahme verweigern	to refuse acceptance, to reject	(Arbeit, Leistung erbringen)	to perform, to accomplish
die Annahme eines Wechsels verweigern	to dishonour/refuse a bill of exchange	(Gerät, System)	to function, to work
in der Annahme, daß	on the assumption/ supposition that	an einer Maschine arbeiten	to operate a machine
Annahme einer Gesetzesvorlage	the passing of a bill	**Arbeiter**	worker
		(körperlich)	labourer

(Bediener)	operator, attendant	den Steuerzuschlag aufheben	to lift/remove the import surcharge
(Facharbeiter)	skilled worker		
ungelernter Arbeiter	unskilled worker, labourer	**ausführen**	
Arbeitskräfte	labour, workforce	(exportieren)	to export
		einen Plan ausführen	to implement a plan
aufheben		einen Auftrag ausführen	to execute/carry out an order
(abschaffen)	to abolish, to remove		
(aufbewahren)	to keep	**Ausgabe**	
(hochheben)	to pick up, to lift, to raise	(von Buch)	edition
		(von Aktie)	issue
eine Blockade aufheben	to lift a blocade	(von Geld)	expense, expenditure
Schranken aufheben	to abolish/lift barriers	(Schalter)	counter

b

Band	band	unter keiner Bedingung	in/under no circumstances, on no condition
(Gurt)	belt		
(Ton-/Datenträger)	tape		
am (Fließ)Band arbeiten	to work on the assembly line	Lieferungs- und Zahlungsbedingungen	terms of delivery and payment
Farbband	ribbon		
Klebeband	adhesive tape	**behandeln**	
		mit ... gegen ... behandeln	to treat with ... for ...
Bank		eine Sache behandeln	to handle a matter
(zum Sitzen)	bench	einen Brief streng vertraulich behandeln	to treat a letter as strictly confidential
(für Geldgeschäfte)	bank		
Bankverbindung	account details	Sie wurde wegen Krebs behandelt.	She was treated for cancer.
bearbeiten			
(eine Sache)	to handle/deal with	**Beruf**	profession, job, occupation
(maschinell)	to machine		
(im Herstellungsgang)	to process	**beruflich**	vocational
(Holz, Metall)	to work on	berufliche Umschulung	vocational rehabilitation
(Buch)	to adapt, to revise	berufliche Weiterbildung	vocational training
(behandeln)	to treat		
einen Auftrag bearbeiten	to process an order	beruflicher Werdegang	professional career
Bearbeitung	handling, machining, treatment, processing	**Berufskrankheit**	occupational/industrial disease
Bedingung		**Besuch**	visit, visiting
(Voraussetzung)	condition	(von Schule, Kurs)	attendance
(Erfordernis)	requirement	einen Besuch abstatten	to pay a visit
(Forderung)	term, condition		
unter der Bedingung, daß	on condition/ with the proviso that	**besuchen**	to visit
		(Schule, Kurs)	to attend

(Person)	to call on, to come to see, to visit
betonen	to point out
(besonders hervorheben)	to emphasize, to stress, to lay/place emphasis on
(Tonfall gebrauchen)	to intonate
Betonung	emphasis, stress, intonation
Betrieb	
(Fabrik)	factory, plant
(Werkstatt)	works, workshop
in Betrieb	in operation/service/action
außer Betrieb	out of operation/service/action
in/außer Betrieb setzen	to put into/out of operation
Streiks zwangen die Betriebsleitung, den Betrieb zu schließen.	Strikes forced the plant management to close the plant.
Bruch	break, breakage
(bildlich)	rupture, breach
(mathematisch)	fraction
(von Knochen)	fracture
diplomatischer Bruch	diplomatic rupture
Bruch von Beziehungen	rupture of relations
Bruch eines Vertrages	breach of a contract
Bruch (Verletzung) eines Abkommens	infringement/violation of a treaty
Bruchlandung	crash-landing
Bruchrechnung	fractions
Bruchschaden	breakage
Bruchstück	fragment
bruchstückhaft	fragmentary
Friedensbruch	breach of the peace

d

Dichtung	
(um abzudichten)	seal, washer
(im Wasserhahn)	washer
(Dichtring)	gasket
(Gedichte)	poetry
(ein Gedicht)	poem
Dienst	
(Arbeit)	work
(Berufsausübung)	duty
(Tätigkeit, Bereich)	service
diplomatischer/öffentlicher Dienst	diplomatic/civil service
zum Dienst gehen	to go to work
im/außer Dienst sein	to be/be not working, to be on/off duty
vom Dienst befreien	to exempt from duty
Dienst tun (bei, als)	to serve (in, as)
den Dienst quittieren	to resign one's post
(beim Militär)	to leave the service
Bereitschaftsdienst	duty
Bereitschaftsdienst haben	to be on call
Druck	
(von drücken)	pressure
(von drucken)	printing
(Gegendruck)	impression
(Kompression)	compression
Druckknopf	
(an Kleid)	press button
(an Maschine)	push button
Druckerzeugnis	printed material
Drucksache	printed matter
Druckzylinder	impression cylinder
drucken	to print
drücken	to press
(stoßen)	to push
(verringern, herabsetzen)	to force down

Einfluß
(Einwirkung) *influence, impact*
(Einströmen) *inflow, influx*
Einfluß haben auf *to have an impact on, to affect*

einführen
(einlegen) *to insert*
(importieren) *to import*
(jemanden vorstellen) *to introduce*
einen Artikel auf dem *to introduce/launch an*
  Markt einführen   *article onto the market*

Einführung *introduction*
(in ein Amt) *installation*

Eingabe
(in Computer) *input*
(Gesuch) *petition*

eingehen
(ankommen) *to arrive, to be received*
(Stoff) *to shrink*
ein Risiko eingehen *to take a risk, to risk*
einen Vergleich ein- *to reach a settlement,*
  gehen   *to settle*
eingegangene Post *mail received*
eingehen auf *to go into sth.*
(zustimmen) *to agree to*
auf einen Vorschlag
  eingehen *to agree to a suggestion*

Einkommen *income*
(Ertrag, Erlös) *profit, returns, proceeds, yield*
(Gehalt) *salary*
(Lohn) *wage, wages*
(Verdienst) *earnings*
(Einnahmen des Staats) *revenue*
pro-Kopf-Einkommen *per capita income, income per head of population*
Einkommensquelle *source of revenue*
Nettoeinkommen *after tax/net earnings, earnings after tax*

einmischen
(sich einsetzen für) *to intervene*
(stören) *to interfere*

Einrichtung
(Anordnung) *arrangement*
(Ausstattung) *equipment*
(Einstellung) *adjustment, setting*
(Gelegenheit) *facility*
(Gründung) *establishment*
(Möbel) *furniture*
(öffentliche) *institution*
(Organisation) *organization*
(Vorrichtung) *device, mechanism, apparatus, appliance*
Freizeiteinrichtung *leisure facilities*

einstellen
(aufgeben) *to discontinue, to stop*
(vorübergehend) *to defer, to postpone*
(einrichten, ausrichten) *to set, to align*
(Leute) *to employ, to engage, to hire*
(technisch) *to adjust*
(Werkzeuge) *to tool*
(Zahlungen) *to suspend*
sich auf etwas *to get ready for*
  einstellen   *something*
Einstellung *setting, alignment, employment, engagement, adjustment, postponement, suspension*
(Haltung) *attitude*
ihre politische/ *her political/religious*
  religiöse Einstellung   *views*
Einstellungsgespräch *interview*

Einzelheiten *details, particulars*
(technische) *data, details*
(Daten zu einer Person) *personal data*

entsprechen
(einem Muster) *to come up to, to be up to, to correspond to,*
(Wünschen) *to meet, to comply with*
einer Sache ent-
  sprechen *to conform to something*
was einem Preis von *which equals a*
  ... entspricht   *price of ...*
$ 1 entspricht ...DM *$ 1 equals DM ..., is equal/equivalent to*

11

entsprechend	corresponding, respective
(gemäß)	in line/accordance with, in obedience to, pursuant to
(übereinstimmend, folgerichtig)	consistent with
(in Übereinstimmung mit)	in compliance/conformity with
entsprechend sein	to be equal/equivalent to, to correspond to
sich entsprechend verhalten	to behave accordingly
erfahren	to learn, to find out
(erleben)	to experience
Veränderungen erfahren	to undergo changes
Erfahrung	experience, practice
(in der Betriebsführung)	management practice
erhalten	
(empfangen)	to receive, to get
(nach Antrag, Mühe)	to obtain
einen Brief erhalten	to receive a letter
eine Lizenz erhalten	to obtain a licence
eine Witwenrente erhalten	to receive a widow's pension
erhöhen	
(anheben)	to raise
(erweitern)	to expand, to enlarge
(verschönern, wertvoller machen)	to enhance
(steigern)	to increase
den Lebensstandard erhöhen	to raise the standard of living
Preise erhöhen	to increase prices
Erhöhung	raising, enhancement, increase, rise
(Hügel)	hill
Lohnerhöhung	rise, [US] raise
Preiserhöhung	increase
erinnern	
sich erinnern	to remember, to recall, to recollect
jemanden an etwas erinnern	to remind someone of something
an etwas erinnern	to commemorate
Erinnerung	memory
(Zahlungserinnerung)	reminder
Das Denkmal wurde zur Erinnerung an Nelsons Sieg erbaut.	This statue was built to commemorate Nelson's victory.
erklären	
(auseinanderlegen)	to explain
(bekanntgeben)	to declare
einem Land den Krieg erklären	to declare war on a country
Erklärung	explanation, declaration
(beim Zoll)	declaration
Steuererklärung	tax return
Erleichterung	facilitation, ease
(Entlastung)	relief
zu ihrer Erleichterung	to her relief
erledigen	to take care of, to deal with
(Auftrag)	to carry out, to execute
(Sache, Rechnung)	to settle
Einkäufe erledigen	to do the shopping
erledigt (Stempel)	dealt with, processed
Erledigung	
(Ausführung)	carrying out, execution
(Durchführung)	completion
(von Sache, Rechnung)	settlement
erreichen	to reach
(Ort)	to arrive at, to get to
(Absicht, Zweck)	to achieve, to attain
(Zug)	to catch
einen hohen Umsatz erreichen	to achieve a high turnover
Ersatz	substitute, replacement
(als Reserve)	spare ...
(Vergütung)	compensation
(von Kosten)	reimbursement
Ersatzteile	spare parts
Schadensersatz	damages
Schadensersatz fordern	to claim damages
ersetzen	to replace
(ablösen)	to supersede
Dieser Auftrag ersetzt unsere Bestellung vom ...	This order supersedes our order dated ...

Fabrik	*factory*
Fabrikanlage	*plant*
Papierfabrik	*paper mill*
Textilfabrik	*textile mill*
Fall	
(das Fallen)	*fall*
(Fallbeispiel)	*instance*
(bildlich)	*fall, downfall*
(Kurse, Temperatur)	*drop, fall*
(Sachverhalt)	*case*
(juristisch, medizinisch)	*case*
(Gelegenheit)	*occasion*
(Grammatik)	*case*
in diesem Fall	*in this case or instance*
in vielen Fällen	*in many instances*
für den Fall, daß sie ...	*in case she ...*
auf jeden Fall	*at any rate*
auf alle Fälle	*in any case*
für solche Fälle	*for such occasions*
falsch	
(fehlerhaft)	*wrong, incorrect*
(irreführend)	*false*
(unaufrichtig)	*false*
(ungeeignet)	*unfit (for)*
falscher Eindruck	*false impression*
ein falscher Name	*an assumed/false name*
Farbe	*colour*
(zum Anstreichen)	*paint*
(zum Drucken)	*ink*
Feder	
(eines Vogels)	*feather*
(technisch)	*spring*
(in Holz)	*tongue*
Fehler	*mistake*
(Irrtum)	*error*
(Schuld)	*fault*
(im Material)	*defect*
(technisch)	*fault*
fest	
(sicher, entschlossen)	*firm*
(nicht beweglich)	*stationary, fixed*
(hart)	*solid*
(nicht locker)	*tight*
(stabil, fig.)	*steady, stable*
(Gewebe, Schuhe)	*tough, sturdy*
ein fester Auftrag	*a firm order*
ein fester Plan	*a definite plan*
fördern	*to promote*
(unterstützen)	*to support*
(finanziell)	*to sponsor, to finance*
(pflegen, begünstigen)	*to foster*
(unterstützen)	*to support*
(weiterbringen)	*to further*
(Bodenschätze)	*to extract, to mine*
Wachstum und Wohlstand fördern	*to foster growth and prosperity*
den Handel fördern	*to further trade*
jemandes Interessen fördern	*to further/advance someone's interests*
den Absatz fördern	*to promote/boost sales*
das Vertrauen der Kunden fördern	*to promote goodwill*
Förderung	*promotion, support, sponsorship, furtherance*
(Kohle, Erz)	*mining*
(Gewinnung)	*extraction*
Form	*form*
(Bauart)	*construction*
(Gestaltungsform)	*shape*
(Gußform, Gießform)	*mould*
(einer Maschine)	*model, design, type*
(Umrisse)	*contours*
in aller Form	*formally*
in guter Form sein	*to be in good form*
in schlechter Form sein	*to be off form*
formen	*to form*
(gestalten)	*to shape*
Formfehler	*irregularity*
Frage	*question*
(Angelegenheit)	*issue*
Fragen stellen	*to ask questions*
fragen	*to ask*
fragen nach	*to ask for*
(befragen)	*to question*
(verhören)	*to interrogate*
Fragestellung	*problem*

frei	*free*	**früher**	*earlier*
(kostenlos)	*free, free of charge, gratis*	(in früheren Zeiten)	*former(ly)*
(leer)	*empty*	(vorhergehend)	*previous*
(liberal)	*liberal*		
(offen)	*open*	**führen**	*to lead, to guide*
(unabhängig)	*free, freelance*	(durchführen)	*to conduct, to run*
(unbesetzt)	*vacant*	(verlaufen)	*to go, to run*
(verfügbar)	*available*	ein Geschäft führen	*to conduct/run a business*
(Fahrt, Blick)	*clear*	ein Orchester führen	*to conduct/lead an orchestra*
Eintritt frei	*admission free*		
freie Fahrt	*a clear run (to)*	eine Werbekampagne durchführen	*to conduct a publicity campaign*
unter freiem Himmel	*in the open air*	einen Namen führen	*to bear a name*
freier Markt	*open market*	wir führen Marken-	*we stock proprietary*
freie Mitarbeiterin sein	*to work/be freelance*	fabrikate	*articles*
freie Stelle	*vacancy*	**Führung**	*guidance, leadership*
freiwillig	*voluntary*	(eines Unternehmens)	*management*
(wahlweise)	*optional*	(Betragen)	*conduct*
ein freiwilliges/nicht angefordertes Angebot	*a voluntary/unsolicited offer*	(Besichtigung)	*guided tour*
sich freiwillig melden	*to volunteer*	(technisch)	*guide, guideway*
Freiwillige(r)	*volunteer*	die Führung übernehmen	*to take the lead*

g

Gang		**Gedächtnis**	
(Spaziergang)	*walk*	(Erinnerungsvermögen)	*memory*
(Ablauf)	*course*	(Gedenken)	*remembrance*
(Arbeitsgang)	*operation*	etwas im Gedächtnis haben	*to keep something in mind*
(Besorgung)	*errand*		
(von Motor)	*running*	aus dem Gedächtnis streichen	*to wipe something out of one's mind*
(Gangart)	*way of walking*		
(eines Gewindes)	*thread*	**geeignet für**	*suitable for*
(in Kirche/Geschäft)	*aisle*	(angemessen)	*appropriate*
(mechanisch)	*gear*	geeignete Maßnahmen	*appropriate measures*
(Speisenfolge)	*course*		
(Bande, Gruppe)	*gang*	**Gefahr**	*danger*
ein 5-Gang Essen	*a 5-course meal*	(Risiko)	*risk, peril*
		(Bedrohung)	*threat*
geboren	*born*	die versicherte Gefahr	*the risk insured against*
er ist geborener Deutscher	*he is German by birth*	**Geheimnis**	*secret*
eine geborene Australierin	*a native of Australia*	(Mysterium)	*mystery*
geborene Schmidt (z.B. im Paß)	*née Schmidt*	**gemeinsam**	*common, joint*
sie ist eine geborene Schmidt	*her maiden name is Schmidt*	(gegenseitig)	*mutual*
zu etwas geboren sein	*to be born to*	etwas gemeinsam haben	*to have something in common*

gemeinsames Konto	joint account	erwarteter Gewinn	anticipated profit
ein gemeinsamer Freund	a mutual friend	Er ist ein großer Gewinn für die Firma.	He is a great asset for our firm.
Gemeinsamer Markt	Common Market	Das ist ein großer Gewinn für mich.	I have gained a lot from this.
genau	exact, accurate	**Bruttogewinn**	gross profit
(präzise)	precise	**gewinnen**	
peinlich genau	meticulous	(siegen)	to win
genau um 19 Uhr	at 7 p.m. sharp, at exactly 7 o'clock	(erwerben, bekommen)	to gain
		(als Profit)	to make a profit of
in genau drei Tagen	in exactly three days	(erzeugen)	to produce, to obtain
		(Erze)	to mine, to extract
Geschäft		an Bedeutung gewinnen	to gain importance
(Gewerbe, Handel)	business		
(Abschluß)	(business) deal, transaction	**gießen**	
		(eingießen)	to pour
(Aufgabe)	duty	(Metall, Plastik, Gips)	to cast
(Firma)	company, office		
(Gewinn)	profit	**Grenze**	
(Laden)	shop, store	(abstrakt)	limit
mit jemandem Geschäfte machen	to do business with someone	(Landesgrenze)	border, frontier
		(natürliche)	boundary
sie haben ein Geschäft gemacht	they made a profit	die Grenze überschreiten	to cross the frontier
geschäftlich	on business	**Staatsgrenze**	state boundary
gesund		**groß**	
(Person)	healthy, well	(breit)	large
(Firma, Ansicht, Urteil)	sound	(dick)	big
(zuträglich)	wholesome	(bildlich)	great
gesunde Beziehungen	sound relations	(riesig)	huge
gesunder Menschenverstand	common sense	(riesig an Fläche)	vast
		(umfangreich)	substantial, considerable
gewähren	to grant		
(zugestehen)	to concede	(wichtig)	important
einen Kredit gewähren	to grant/extend a credit	ein großer Auftrag	a substantial/big/large order
einen Vorschuß gewähren	to advance money	große Nachfrage	considerable demand
		großer Reichtum	great wealth
Gewinn	profit	mit großen Schwierigkeiten	with great difficulties
(Vorteil)	benefit	**Größe**	
(Erlös)	proceeds	(Format, Maßeinheit)	size
(Ertrag, Rendite)	yield	(Ausmaß)	extent
(Ertrag, Umsatz)	return	(bildlich)	greatness
(Preis, Treffer)	prize	(Körpergröße)	height
(bildlich: Vorteil)	gain	(Fläche)	area, size, dimension(s)

h

halten	
(in Position)	*to hold*
(tragen, stützen)	*to hold up, to support, to bear*
(bildlich: behalten)	*to keep*
(abhalten)	*to give, to hold*
(erfüllen)	*to keep*
Waren behalten	*to keep/retain goods*
im Gleichgewicht halten	*to keep in balance*
eine Rede halten	*to hold/make/deliver a speech*
Unterricht halten	*to give/hold lessons*
sein Versprechen halten	*to keep one's promise*
Handel	
(Geschäft)	*business/transaction/deal*
(Handelsverkehr)	*trade, commerce*
Handel treiben	*to do business*
in den Handel bringen	*to put on the market*
nicht mehr im Handel sein	*to be off/no longer on the market*
Handels- ...	*commercial ...*
handeltreibend	*trading*
Handelsgesellschaft	*trading company*
Tauschhandel	*barter*
handeln	
(tätig werden)	*to act*
(Handel treiben)	*to trade*
(um Preis feilschen)	*to bargain*
(handeln mit)	*to deal in*
(handeln von)	*to deal with*
Handlung	
(Tat)	*act*
(Geschehen)	*action*
(Geschäft)	*business, shop*
(eines Romans, Films)	*action, story*
(Handlungsverlauf)	*plot*

k

Kanal	*channel*
(künstlich)	*canal*
(Radio, Fernsehen)	*channel*
(Abwasserkanal)	*sewer*
Ärmelkanal	*the English Channel*
Kasse	
(Bargeld)	*cash*
(Geldbehälter)	*cashbox*
(Krankenkasse)	*medical/health insurance company*
(Sparkasse)	*(savings) bank*
(Zahlstelle)	*cashpoint, cashdesk, till*
(im Supermarkt)	*check out*
Kasse gegen Dokumente	*cash against documents*
knapp bei Kasse sein	*to be short of cash, to be hard up*
kaum	
(schwerlich)	*hardly, scarcely*
(nur gerade)	*barely*
(mit Mühe)	*with difficulty*
kaum je	*hardly ever*
kaum glaublich	*hard to believe*
kaum hatte er ... als	*no sooner had he ... than, hardly had he ... when*
wohl kaum!	*hardly!, most unlikely*
Keil	
(spitzwinklig)	*wedge*
(an Maschine)	*key*
Keilriemen	*drive belt, V-belt*
(Auto)	*fan belt*
Kissen	
(Kopfkissen)	*pillow*
(Polster)	*cushion*
(bildlich)	*cushion*
Luftkissen	*air cushion*
Kiste	*case*
(Karton, Kasten)	*box*
(Lattenkiste, Holzverschlag)	*crate*
(Teekiste)	*chest*

klein	*little, small*	**Nebenkosten**	*incidental costs*
(gering)	*minor*	**kündigen**	
(geringfügig)	*slight*	(durch Arbeit-	
		nehmer oder Mieter)	*to hand in/give in one's notice*
Kontrolle		(durch Vermieter)	*to give someone notice*
(Aufsicht)	*supervision, control*		*to quit*
(Aufsichtsperson)	*supervisor, controller*	(Mitgliedschaft)	*to cancel, to disconti-*
(Beherrschung)	*control*		*nue, to terminate*
(Überprüfung)	*check*	(Vertrag)	*to terminate*
(Überwachung)	*monitoring, surveillance*	jemandem die Stellung	*to give someone his/her*
Kontrolle ausüben	*to exercise control*	kündigen	*notice*
Kontrollinstrumente	*controlling instruments/*	**Kündigung**	*notice, dismissal, can-*
	mechanisms/devices		*cellation, termination*
Kontrollproben	*checks, samples*	(von Anleihe)	*withdrawal*
Kontrollsysteme	*checking systems*	**Kupplung**	
Paßkontrolle	*passport control*	(Schaltkupplung)	*clutch*
Zollkontrolle	*customs examination*	(Verbindungs-	
kontrollieren		kupplung)	*coupling*
(beherrschen)	*to control*	die Kupplung durch-	
(beaufsichtigen)	*to supervise*	treten	*to disengage the clutch*
(prüfen)	*to check*		
		kurz	*short*
Kosten	*cost, costs*	(zeitlich)	*brief, short*
(Aufwand)	*expenditure*	kurz beschreiben	*to describe in brief*
(Ausgaben)	*expenses*	**Kürze**	*shortness*
(Gebühren)	*charges, fees*	in Kürze	*shortly, soon*
auf Ihre Kosten	*at your expense*	**kürzlich**	*recent(ly)*
Kostenfrage	*question of cost*		
kostenlos	*free of charge, gratis*		

l

Land	*land*	(Unterricht)	*instruction*
(Einzelstaat)	*country, state*	(Warnung)	*warning*
auf dem Land	*in the country*	(Meßgerät)	*gauge*
einen Auftrag an Land		Lehre von	*science of*
ziehen	*to land/win a contract*		
Bundesland	*state, land of the FRG*	**leihen**	
		(borgen, ausleihen)	*to borrow*
laufend	*running*	(verleihen)	*to lend*
(augenblicklich gültig)	*current*	Geld bei einer Bank	*to borrow money from/*
		leihen	*raise a loan with a bank*
Lehre			
(Lektion)	*lesson*	**Leistung**	
(Ratschlag)	*advice*	(abgegebene)	*output*
(beim Handwerk)	*apprenticeship*	(aufgenommene)	*input*
(das Lehren)	*teaching*	(von Dampfmaschine,	
(Nutzanwendung)	*moral*	Motor)	*power*
(theoretische)	*doctrine*	(Haltbarkeit)	*(service) life*

(Leistungsfähigkeit)	*capacity*		**lösen**	
(eines Menschen)	*efficiency, achievement, accomplishment*		(abmachen)	*to remove*
			(Problem)	*to solve*
(einer Maschine)	*efficiency*		(auflösen)	*to dissolve*
(Produktion)	*output*		(Karte)	*to buy, to get*
			(Schraube)	*to loosen, to unscrew*
liefern			(Vertrag)	*to cancel*
(beliefern)	*to supply*		**unlösbar** (Problem)	*insoluble*
(zustellen)	*to deliver*		**Lösung**	
(zur Verfügung stellen)	*to supply*		(Auflösung)	*dissolution*
(Ertrag)	*to yield*		(Lösungsmittel)	*solvent*
(Beweise, Information)	*to provide, to furnish*		(einer Schraube)	*loosening, unscrewing*
Merke: *to supply someone with something, to deliver something to someone*			(eines Vertrages)	*cancellation*
			die Lösung des Problems	*the solution to the problem*

m

Marke			**mieten**	
(Briefmarke)	*stamp*		(ein Haus)	*to rent*
(einer Ware)	*brand*		(ein Auto)	*to hire, to rent*
(Automarke)	*make*		(pachten, im Leasingverfahren)	*to lease, to take on lease*
(Type)	*type*			
(Zeichen)	*mark*		**Mieter**	*tenant*
(für Automaten)	*token*		(Untermieter)	*lodger*
Fabrikmarke	*manufacturer's brand*		**vermieten**	*to lease, to let*
Handelsmarke	*dealer's brand*		ein Haus vermieten	*to let (out) a house*
Markenartikel	*trade-marked goods, branded articles*		**Mitte**	
			(Mittelpunkt)	*centre*
Markenname	*brand name*		(räumlich)	*middle*
Markenschutz	*protection of trade marks*		(zeitlich)	*middle or mid*
			bis Mitte Januar	*by the middle of January, by mid-January*
Markenware	*branded article, proprietary article*			
Markenzeichenschutz	*trade mark registration*		auf der Mitte des Weges	*half-way, midway*
Maschine	*machine*		**Mittel**	*means*
(Flugzeug)	*plane*		(chemische Mischung)	*compound, agent*
(Motor)	*engine, motor*		(finanzielle)	*means, funds, resources*
Maschinenbau	*mechanical engineering*		(Maßnahme)	*measure*
Verbrennungsmaschine	*combustion engine*		(Durchschnitt)	*average*
Schreibmaschine	*typewriter*		(Vorrichtung)	*device*
			Heilmittel	*remedy, medicine*
Menge			**mittelgroß**	*medium-sized*
(Masse)	*mass*		**mittelmäßig**	*mediocre*
(Menschenmenge)	*crowd*		**mittels**	*by means of*
(Quantität)	*quantity*		**mittig**	*centrally (aligned)*
eine Menge	*a lot, lots of*			

mittler			**Verbrennungsmotor**	*internal combustion engine*
mittlere Qualität	*average/medium/fair average quality*		**Muster**	
Personen mittleren Alters	*middle-aged people*		(Musterstück)	*sample*
Motor			(Dessin)	*pattern*
(elektrisch)	*motor*		(Modell, Musterexemplar)	*model, specimen*
(mit Brennstoff arbeitend)	*engine*		**Musterbeispiel**	*perfect example*
(im Auto)	*automobile/car engine*		**Musterbrief**	*specimen/model letter*

n

Nachteil	*disadvantage*		**netto**	
(Hindernis, Haken)	*drawback*		(bei Gewicht)	*net*
(Schaden)	*damage*		(bei Einkommen)	*after tax, net*
(juristisch)	*prejudice, detriment*		**Nettopreis**	*net price*
(Verlust)	*loss*			
zum Nachteil (Schaden) von	*to the detriment of*		**nur** (bloß)	*only, just* *merely*
zum Nachteil (auf Kosten) von	*at the expense of*		nur zur Information	*only/merely for information*

o

offen			**offenbleiben**	*to stay open*
(auch bildlich)	*open*		**offenhalten**	*to keep open*
(frei heraus)	*frank*			
offen gesagt	*frankly speaking*		**Opfer**	
offenes Konto/offene Rechnung	*outstanding account*		(Verzicht) (Person)	*sacrifice* *victim*
offene Stelle	*vacancy*		(Beute)	*prey*

p

Päckchen	*small parcel*		**Packung, Verpackung**	*packaging*
(Schachtel)	*pack, packet*		Kosten für Verpackung	*cost for packing*
(Bündel)	*packet, bundle*		**Verpackungsindustrie**	*packaging industry*
Paket				
(Postpaket)	*parcel*		**Pause**	
(Packung)	*packet*		(Ruhepause)	*rest*
(abgepackte Menge)	*package*		(bei der Arbeit)	*break*
(Sammlung)	*packet*		(im Gang der Handlung)	*pause, interlude*
Paketpost	*parcel post*		(Unterbrechung)	*interruption*

(im Theater)	interval
Sie machten drei Tage Pause.	They took a three days' rest.
Sie genossen ihre Teepause.	They enjoyed their tea break.
Person	person
(Einzelperson)	individual
(im Theater)	character
Personen (Leute)	people
Personal	personnel, staff
Personalchef	staff manager
persönlich	personal
Pflicht	
(Aufgabe)	duty, task
Pflicht-...	compulsory ...
Pflichtanteil	quota
Pflichtmitgliedschaft	compulsory membership
Pflichtteil	legal portion
Verpflichtung	liability, obligation
Plan	plan
(Programm)	programme
(Stadtplan)	map/town plan
(Zeitplan)	schedule, timetable
Wartungsplan	maintenance programme
Platz	
(Sitzplatz)	seat
(in einem Kurs)	place
(Raum)	space
(in einem Koffer)	space, room
(Ort, Stelle)	place
(umbaute Fläche)	square
(Standort)	position
(Bauplatz)	site
(Stellung, Rang)	place
ein freier Platz	a clear space
einen Platz reservieren	to reserve a seat
Platz schaffen für	to make room for
Golfplatz	golf course
Sportplatz	field, ground
Tennisplatz	tennis court
Post	
(Schriftstücke)	mail, post, letters
(Postamt)	post office
mit gleicher Post	by the same post/mail
mit separater Post	under separate cover

Prämie	premium
(Preis)	award, prize
(bei Versicherung)	rate
Preis	
(den man zahlt)	price
(den man gewinnt)	prize
einen Preis verleihen	to award a prize
um jeden Preis	at any cost/price
Probe	
(Test)	test
(Erprobung)	trial
(Kontrollprobe)	check
(Musterstück)	sample, specimen
(Experiment)	experiment
(Probedruck)	proof
auf Probe	on probation/trial
Probebelastung	proof load/weight, test load, stress test
Probejahr	year of probation, probationary year
Probelauf	test run
probeweise	on a trial basis
Probezeit	probation
Prospekt	brochure, folder
(Werbezettel)	leaflet
(Broschüre, Flugschrift)	brochure, pamphlet
(Katalog)	catalogue
(wirtschaftlich)	prospectus
Zur Verwendung siehe auch Seite 55	
Prozeß	
(juristisch)	lawsuit, action
(Gerichtsverfahren)	trial
(Rechtsfall)	court case
(Verfahren, Vorgehensweise)	procedure, proceedings
(Vorgang)	process
einen Prozeß anstrengen	to take legal proceedings, to sue
einen Prozeß mit jemandem haben	to be involved in/ carry on a lawsuit with someone
es zum Prozeß kommen lassen	to go to court
der Prozeß Schmidt gegen Schmidt	the case of Schmidt versus Schmidt

prüfen	to check	die Preise prüfen	to examine the prices
(Nachforschungen anstellen)	to investigate	Merke: prüfen nie mit *to prove* übersetzen, das bedeutet beweisen, sich erweisen.	
(untersuchen)	to examine	**Prüfung**	check, checking,
(testen, ausprobieren)	to test		examination, test,
(überwachen)	to survey, to control		control, trial,
(versuchen)	to try		verification, inspection
(auf Richtigkeit)	to verify	nach Prüfung	after verification/ checking
ein Angebot prüfen	to study an offer		
die Qualität prüfen	to test the quality	zur Prüfung einschicken	to send for inspection

q

Quelle		aus guter (zuverlässiger) Quelle	from reliable sources
(Brunnen)	well	**Quellenangabe**	reference
(Ursprung)	source	**Quellensteuer**	tax deducted at source
(Wasser)	spring, fountain, source		

r

Rad	wheel	**Rechnung**	
(verzahnt)	gear	(in Restaurant oder Hotel)	bill
(Autoreifen)	tyre	(kaufmännisch)	invoice
(Fahrrad)	bicycle, bike	(Berechnung)	calculation
Lenkrad	steering wheel		
Kettenrad	sprocket (wheel/gear)	**Rechtsanwalt**	lawyer
		(Anwalt, Sachwalter)	solicitor
Rat		(an höheren Gerichten zugelassen)	barrister
(Ratschlag, Ratschläge)	advice [kein Plural]	Wir werden die Angelegenheit unseren Anwälten übergeben.	We shall hand the matter over to our solicitors.
(Ratsversammlung)	council		
(Beratung, Rechtsbeistand)	counsel		
(Person)	senior official	**Reihe**	
Ratgeber	adviser	(Aufeinanderfolge)	succession
(Buch)	guide	(hintereinander)	file
Rathaus	town hall	(nebeneinander)	rank
Ratschlag	piece of advice	(eine Linie)	line, row, range
raten		(mathematisch)	progression
(erraten, schätzen)	to guess	(Menschenschlange)	queue
(beraten)	to advise	(Palette von Produkten)	range
		(Serie)	series
Raum		(Sitzreihe)	tier, row
(Zimmer)	room	**Häuserreihe**	row of houses
(Bereich, räumlich)	area	**Reihen- ...**	series ...
(Bereich, bildlich)	sphere	**Reihenfabrikation**	series/serial production
(Platz)	space, room		
(Spielraum)	room, scope		

Reihen-/Seriennummer	serial number
Reihenfolge	sequence, order, succession
reihenweise	in series
Sie wurden reihenweise ohnmächtig.	They fainted by the dozen.
Reise	journey
(Ausflug)	excursion
(Tour)	trip
(Seereise)	voyage
Dienstreise	business trip
reisen	to travel
(in den Urlaub)	to go on holiday
Reisender	
(Fahrgast)	passenger
(geschäftlich)	(commercial) traveller, travelling salesman
Rest	rest
(Rückstand)	residue
Rest einer Schuld	remainder of a debt
Reste (Überbleibsel)	remains
Restbestand, Restbetrag	remainder
Riß	
(Bruch)	fracture, breakage
(geologisch)	crevasse
(Grundriß)	plan
(Zeichnung)	design
(konstruktionstechnisch)	draft
(Haarriß)	hairline crack
(Leck)	leakage
(Sprung in Gußstücken)	crack
(Kratzer)	scratch
(im Stoff)	tear, rent
(Uneinigkeit, Bruch)	breach
(Wunde)	laceration
Roh- ...	raw, crude, rough
rohe Behandlung	rough handling
Rohbaumwolle	raw cotton
Rohmaterial	raw material
Rohöl	crude oil
Ruf	
(Aufruf)	call
(Ansehen)	reputation
(Fernruf)	telephone number
(Universität: Berufung)	offer of a chair

S

Satz	
(aus Wörtern)	sentence
(Bausatz)	kit
(im Tennis)	set
(im Musikstück)	movement
(passende Teile)	set
Schaden	
(Beschädigung)	damage [kein Plural]
(Defekt)	fault
(körperlicher Mangel)	defect
(Personenschaden)	injury
(Verlust)	loss
(Unheil)	harm
Schadenersatz	damages [kein Singular]
Schadenersatz fordern	to claim damages
schaffen	
(schöpferisch)	to create
(verursachen)	to cause, to create
(eine Sache)	to manage to do something, to succeed in doing something
schalten	
(elektrisch)	to switch, to connect, to wire up
(steuern)	to control
(einrücken)	to engage
(ausrücken)	to disengage
nebeneinander schalten	to connect in parallel
in Reihe schalten	to connect in series
ausschalten	to switch/turn off, to cut out, to break
einen Motor ausschalten	to switch off/cut out a motor
einen Stromkreis ausschalten	to break a circuit
einschalten	to switch/turn on

Schalter	switch	Tagschicht	day-shift
Schaltschema	wiring diagram	vielschichtig	multilayered
Schaltschrank	switch cabinet	(bildlich)	complex
Schalttafel	switchboard		
Schaltung	circuit, wiring system	**Schuld**	
(im Auto)	manual gear change	(Fehler)	fault
		(finanzielle Ver-	obligations, commit-
schätzen		pflichtungen)	ments
(abschätzen)	to estimate, to assess	(Geldschuld)	debt(s)
(Wertgegenstand)	to value	(Religion)	sin
(etwas begrüßen)	to appreciate, to value	(Strafbarkeit)	guilt
(damit rechnen)	to reckon, to guess	**Schuldschein**	promissory note, IOU
jemanden schätzen	to regard someone highly	**Schuldverschreibung**	debenture bond
		schuldig	guilty
an unsere geschätzten Kunden	to our esteemed customers	**schuldlos**	innocent
		Schuldner	debtor
Ich schätze Ihre Stellungnahme.	I appreciate/value your comments.	**schwer**	
		(an Gewicht)	heavy
Schätzung	estimate	(ernstlich)	serious
(das Schätzen)	estimation	(schwerwiegend)	severe, grave
(von Wertgegenständen)	valuation	(schwierig)	difficult
		ein schwerer Schlag	a heavy blow
Scheibe	disc, disk	die schwere Rezession	the severe recession
(Brot)	slice	eine schwere Straftat	a grave offence
(die man abschneidet)	cut, slice	schwer angegriffen	
(dünnes Plättchen)	lamella	(krank) sein	to be gravely affected
(Glasscheibe)	pane		
Dichtungsscheibe	gasket	**Sicherheit**	safety, security
Riemenscheibe	pulley	(Gegenteil von Gefahr)	safety
Seilscheibe	sheave	(Gewißheit)	certainty
Unterlegscheibe	washer	(Pfand)	surety
Wählscheibe	dial	(wirtschaftlich)	security
Zielscheibe	target	(Zuverlässigkeit)	reliability
		Sicherheit leisten	to offer security
Schicht			
(Arbeitsschicht)	shift	**Sorgfalt**	care
(Arbeiterkolonne)	gang	**sorgfältig**	
(geologisch)	layer	(aufmerksam)	attentive
(Niederschlag, Boden- satz)	sediment	(genau)	exact, accurate
		(gewissenhaft)	concentious
(dünne)	coating, film, veneer	(übergenau)	meticulous
(Gesellschaftsschicht)	rank, class	(vorsichtig)	careful, cautious
(Stapel)	pile	**Sorgfältigkeit**	carefulness
die unteren Schichten	the lower classes		
aus allen Schichten der Bevölkerung	from all walks of life	**Spalte**	
		(in der Zeitung)	column
Ölschicht	oil film	(Riß, Kluft)	gap
Nachtschicht	night-shift	(Felsspalte)	crevice
Schichtarbeit	shift-work	(Gletscherspalte)	crevasse
Schichtseite (Foto)	emulsion side		

Spannung	
(Dehnung)	*tension*
(Anspannung, Anstrengung)	*strain*
(elastische)	*stress*
(gespanntes Verhältnis)	*tension*
(Strom)	*voltage, tension*
(von Gasen, Druck)	*pressure*
(Aufregung)	*excitement*
Speicher	
(Behälter)	*reservoir, tank*
(Computer)	*memory*
(Dachboden)	*loft, attic*
(Lagerhaus)	*storehouse*
Spiel	*game*
(Theateraufführung)	*performance, play*
(Toleranz)	*play, clearance*
(bei Rädern, Ketten)	*slackness, play*
(Schlupf, toter Gang)	*backlash*
Spitze	*tip, point*
(einer Belastung)	*peak*
(eines Berges)	*peak, summit, top*
(oberste Spitze)	*top*
(Stoff)	*lace*
Brüsseler Spitze	*lace from Brussels*
Spitzenbelastung	*peak/maximum load*
stabil	
(stark)	*strong, sturdy, rigid*
(bildlich)	*stable*
(fest)	*firm, steady*
die Währung stabil halten	*to keep the currency stable*
Stabilität	*stability*
Stand	*stand*
(Beruf, Gewerbe)	*profession*
(Klasse)	*rank, class*
(Lage)	*state*
(Niveau)	*level*
(Messestand)	*stand, booth*
(Position)	*position*
(das Stehen)	*standing position*
(von Thermometer)	*reading, level*
(soziale Stellung)	*station, status*
standfest	*stable*
Standort	*position, location*

Stelle	*place, spot*
(zeitlich, bildlich)	*point*
(Behörde)	*authority*
(Dienststelle)	*office*
(freie Stelle)	*vacancy*
(Lage, Platz)	*place*
(Posten)	*job*
an dieser Stelle,	
(örtlich)	*in this place, on this spot*
(zeitlich)	*at this point*
an geeigneter Stelle	*at an appropriate moment*
eine schwache Stelle	*a weak point*
anstelle von	*instead of, in place of*
still	
(ruhig)	*quiet*
(Wetter)	*calm*
(schweigsam)	*silent*
ein stiller Teilhaber	*a sleeping partner*
Stille	*quietness, calmness, silence*
still-...	*still*
stillstehen	*to stand still*
Stillstand	*standstill*
Stimme	*voice*
(bei Abstimmung)	*vote*
abstimmen	*to vote*
einstimmig	*unanimous*
stören	*to disturb*
(belästigen)	*to bother*
(Handlungsablauf)	*to disrupt*
(Radio etc.)	*to jam*
Störung	
(auch bildlich)	*disturbance*
(elektrisch)	*interference*
(technisch)	*fault, malfunction*
(Unannehmlichkeit)	*trouble*
(Unterbrechung)	*interruption*
eine Störung im Außenhandel	*a disturbance in foreign trade*
Streit	*quarrel, argument, dispute*
(Rechtsstreit)	*lawsuit, litigation*
Handelsstreitigkeit	*commercial dispute*
Streitwert	*amount in dispute*

streiten	*to quarrel*		(forschen)	*to search, to research*
(argumentieren über)	*to argue/dispute (about)*		(schauen nach)	*to look for*
(prozessieren)	*to take legal action, to sue*		(trachten nach)	*to seek*
			Arbeit suchen	*to look for a job*
(kämpfen)	*to fight*		Sie suchen einen Weg, die Lage zu verbessern.	*They seek to improve their situation.*
suchen	*to seek*		Kellnerin gesucht	*waitress wanted*
(durchsuchen)	*to search*		**Sucher** (Foto)	*viewfinder*

t

Technik	*technic, technics*
(Verfahren)	*technique*
(Technologie)	*technology*
(Wissenschaft, Studienfach)	*engineering*
technisch	*technical, technological*
technische Fortschritte	*technological progress*
technischer Ausdruck	*technical term*
technische Assistentin	*technical assistant*
Termin	*date*
(zur Besprechung)	*appointment*
(Liefertag)	*delivery date*
(juristisch)	*hearing*
(letzter Termin)	*deadline*
teuer	
(nicht billig)	*expensive*
(lieb)	*dear*
tief	*deep*
(tiefgreifend)	*profound*
(Schmerz, Gefühl)	*intense*
(Wolken, Ausschnitt)	*low*
tief enttäuscht	*deeply disappointed*
Tiefdruck	
(Wetter)	*low pressure*
(Druckwesen)	*gravure printing*
Tiefe	*depth*
(bildlich)	*profundity, deepness*

tragen	
(befördern)	*to carry*
(stützen)	*to support*
(Kleidung)	*to wear*
(einen Bart, ein Gebiß)	*to have*
das Risiko/die Kosten tragen	*to bear the risk/cost*
sich mit einer Idee tragen	*to contemplate an idea*
man trägt wieder kurze Röcke	*short skirts are in fashion*
ertragen	*to stand, to endure, to suffer, to bear*
Ich kann ihn nicht ertragen.	*I can't stand him.*
Träger	
(Holz, Beton)	*(supporting) beam*
(Eisen, Stahl)	*girder*
(Stütze)	*support*
(Flugzeugträger)	*(aircraft) carrier*
(von Lasten)	*bearer, porter*
(Befürworter)	*supporter, upholder*
(von Namen)	*bearer*
(von Kleidung)	*wearer*
(an Wäsche, Kleid)	*strap*
(einer Veranstaltung)	*sponsor*
Tragetasche	*carrier bag*
tragfähig	*able to take a weight*
eine tragfähige Mehrheit	*a workable majority*

Übernahme	*takeover*
(das Übernehmen)	*taking over*
(einer Ansicht)	*adoption*
(eines Amtes)	*assumption*
(Annahme)	*acceptance*
übernehmen	*to take over*
eine Vertretung übernehmen	*to take over an agency*
Verantwortung übernehmen	*to assume responsibility*
übertragen	
(weiterleiten)	*to pass on*
(an andere Stelle bringen)	*to transfer*
(technisch)	*to transmit*
(übersetzen)	*to translate, to render into*
(anwenden)	*to apply to*
(auf Band)	*to tape, to record*
(senden)	*to transmit*
(TV)	*to broadcast on television, to televise*
im übertragenen Sinne	*in a figurative sense*
üblich	
(so wie man es kennt)	*customary*
(gewöhnlich)	*usual*
(üblicherweise)	*usually*
wie üblich/gewöhnlich	*as usual*
Übung	
(häufige Anwendung)	*practice*
(zur Ertüchtigung)	*exercise* [kein Plural]
zur Übung/übungshalber	*for practice*
Grammatikübung	*grammar exercise*
Übungssache	*matter of practice*
Umschlag	
(Briefumschlag)	*envelope*
(Buch)	*jacket*
(Hülle)	*cover*
(medizinisch)	*compress*
(Schallplatte)	*jacket, sleeve*
(Verpackung)	*wrapping*
(umgeschlagene Gütermenge)	*volume of traffic*
(Umladung)	*transfer, transshipment*
ungültig	*invalid*
(abgelaufen)	*expired*
(Münze)	*not current*
(bei Dokumenten)	*void*
unterhalten	
(versorgen)	*to support*
(Angestellte)	*to maintain*
(betreiben)	*to run*
(instandhalten)	*to maintain*
(pflegen, aufrechterhalten)	*to maintain*
(sprechen)	*to talk*
(sich vergnügen)	*to enjoy oneself*
(Gäste)	*to entertain*
(darunterhalten)	*to hold underneath*
unterstützen	*to support*
(helfen)	*to assist*
(fördern)	*to promote*
Unterstützung	*support*
(Hilfe)	*assistance*
(finanziell, vom Staat)	*benefit, allowance*
(Förderung)	*promotion*
Unterstützung zur Verkaufsförderung	*promotional support*
staatliche Unterstützung	*state aid*
Arbeitslosenunterstützung	*unemployment benefit*
Urlaub	*holiday*
(bei Militär)	*leave*
(im Parlament)	*recess*
in Urlaub sein	*to be on holiday/leave/in recess*

V

Verabredung
(mit Freund/in) *date*
(Termin) *appointment*
Ich habe eine Verab- *I have an appointment*
redung mit meinem *with my business*
Geschäftsfreund. *partner.*

verbessern
(abändern) *to amend*
(korrigieren) *to correct*
(besser machen) *to improve*
(verändern) *to modify*
eine verbesserte
 Rechnung *an amended invoice*
Fehler verbessern *to correct errors/mistakes*
Die Lage verbessert *The situation is chang-*
 sich. *ing for the better.*
Verbesserung *amendment, modification*
 correction, improvement

Verbindungen
(Beziehungen) *relations, connections*
(mechanische) *connections*
berufliche Verbin- *professional*
 dungen *connections, contacts*
geschäftliche Verbin- *business relations,*
 dungen *contacts*

verfolgen
(beobachten) *to watch, to observe*
(besonders religiös) *to persecute*
(nachfassen) *to follow up*
(nachjagen) *to hunt*
(strafrechtlich) *to prosecute*
(Idee, Plan) *to pursue*

Vergleich
(von Dingen/Personen) *comparison*
(Schlichtung) *conciliation*
(Einigung) *settlement*
einen Vergleich
 schließen *to reach an agreement*

Verhältnis
(mathematisch) *ratio*
(Anteil) *proportion*
(Beziehung) *relationship*
(Einstellung) *attitude*

Verhältnisse *conditions, circum-*
 stances
bei normalen Verhält- *under normal circum-*
 nissen *stances*
Verhältniswort *preposition*

Verkäufer *seller*
(juristisch) *vendor*
(Einzelhändler) *retailer*
(Großhändler) *wholesaler*
(Angestellter im Laden) *shopassistant*
(Geschäftsreisender) *salesman, salesperson*
(Verkaufspersonal) *sales people, sales force*

Verlängerung
(Ausdehnung) *extension*
(zeitlich) *prolongation*
(von Paß) *renewal*
(Kabel, Schnur) *extension (lead)*
Verlängerung eines *prolongation of a bill*
 Wechsels *of exchange*
Verlängerung des
 Krediets um drei *a three months'*
 Monate *extension of credit*

verletzen
(verwunden) *to injure*
(bildlich) *to wound*
(Ehre) *to hurt*
(Gesetz) *to offend*
(Rechte) *to break*
 to violate

Vermögen
(Reichtum) *fortune, wealth*
(Besitz) *property*
(Fähigkeit) *capacity*
(Können) *ability*
(Macht) *power*
(bildlich) *assets*

Vernunft *reason*
gegen alle Vernunft *contrary to all common*
 sense

vernünftig *sensible*
(rational) *rational*
(sinnvoll, auch bild-
 lich) *reasonable*
(ordentlich, richtig) *properly*

verpflichten
(einstellen) — to engage
(binden) — to commit
(moralisch) — to oblige
(durch Vertrag) — to bind
sich zu etwas ver- — to commit onself to
 pflichten — doing something
Wir sind Ihnen zu Dank
 verpflichtet. — We are obliged to you.
Verpflichtung
(auch moralisch) — commitment
(das Verpflichten) — engagement
(vertragliche Bindung) — engagement
(Verbindlichkeiten) — liabilities
(Zahlungsverpflichtung) — obligation
Verpflichtung zu
 Qualität — commitment to quality
gesellschaftliche Ver- — social engagements,
 pflichtungen — commitments

verrechnen
(begleichen) — to settle
(auszahlen) — to pay out
(belasten) — to debit
(gutschreiben) — to credit
(Gutschein) — to redeem
(Scheck) — to clear
(gegeneinander auf- — to balance something
 rechnen) — with something, to off-
   set something against
   something
(Rechenfehler) — to make a mistake
(falsch berechnen) — to miscalculate

versäumen
(nicht tun) — to fail
(unterlassen) — to omit
(vergeuden, verwirken) — to lose
(den Zug) — to miss the train
Sie versäumten es, den — They failed to acknow-
 Auftrag zu bestätigen. — ledge our order.
Versäumnis
(Fehler) — failing
(Nachlässigkeit) — omission

verschieden
(mehrere) — various, several
(verschiedenartig) — different
(vermischt, vielseitig) — miscellaneous
verschiedene Gläubiger — sundry creditors

„Verschiedenes" — 'miscellaneous'
 (auf Tagesordnung) — 'any other business'
an Verschiedene
 (bei Buchführung) — to Sundries

verschlechtern — to deteriorate
die Sache verschlechtern — to worsen the matter
sich verschlechtern — to get worse/to change
   for the worse
Verschlechterung — deterioration,
   worsening
(Rückgang) — decline
(finanziell) — setback

versichern
(zusichern) — to assure
(garantieren) — to guarantee
(gegen) — to insure
(sich vergewissern) — to make sure or certain
Ich versichere Ihnen, — I assure you that ...,
 daß ... — I guarantee that ...
gegen Transportverlust — to insure against loss in
 versichern — transit
Versicherung
(Zusicherung) — assurance
(die man abschließt) — insurance
Lebensversicherung — life assurance or
   insurance

Versuch
(Anstrengung) — endeavour, effort
(Test, Ausprobieren) — test
(Bemühung) — attempt
(Experiment) — experiment
(Probe) — trial
einen Versuch machen — to try, to have a try
Versuchsanlage — pilot plant/project
versuchen — to try
(sich bemühen) — to attempt
(experimentieren) — to experiment
(testen) — to test

Vertrag
(Vereinbarung) — agreement
(gegengezeichnet) — contract
(zwischen Staaten) — treaty
die Römischen
 Verträge — the Treaties of Rome
Kaufvertrag — contract of sale
Vertretervertrag — agency contract

vertraut		**vollständig**	*complete, full, entire*
vertraut sein mit		(uneingeschränkt)	*entire*
(etwas kennen)	*to be familiar with*	(voll und ganz)	*whole*
(eng)	*to be on intimate terms with*	Die Lager sind vollständig erschöpft.	*The stock is completely exhausted.*
		nicht vollständig	*incomplete*
Verzug	*delay*		
in Verzug sein bei der Zahlung	*to be in arrears with payment*	**Vorgang**	
in Verzug geraten	*to default on, to fall into arrears with*	(Ereignis)	*event, occurrence*
		(Ablauf)	*series/course of events*
		(chemisch)	*process*
Lieferverzug	*delay in delivery*	(Akten)	*file, dossier*

W

Wahl	*choice*	**Wert**	*value*
(Auswahl, Auslese)	*selection*	(von Banknoten)	*denomination*
(politisch)	*election*	(besonders menschlich)	*worth*
Allgemeine Wahlen	*General Election*	(bildlich)	*quality*
nach Wahl		Wert legen auf	*to attach importance to*
(wahlweise) - (nach Belieben)	*optional(ly) at choice*	**wesentlich**	
keine andere Wahl haben als ...	*to have no choice/ option/alternative but...*	(beträchtlich)	*considerable, substantial*
erste Wahl	*top quality/class*	(wichtig)	*essential*
wählen	*to choose*	Es gelang ihnen, den Umsatz wesentlich zu steigern.	*They succeeded in increasing their turnover substantially.*
(auswählen)	*to select*	es wäre uns wesentlich wichtiger...	*we would much rather ...*
(politisch)	*to elect*		
(stimmen für)	*to vote for*		
(mit Wählscheibe)	*to dial*	**wichtig**	*important*
		(unbedingt erforderlich)	*essential*
Währung	*currency*	(absolut notwendig)	*imperative, absolutely necessary*
in deutscher Währung	*in German currency*	(hauptsächlich)	*major*
Goldwährung	*gold standard*	sorgfältige Verpackung ist wichtig	*careful packing is essential/important*
Währungs-...	*monetary*	das Wichtige	*the essentials*
Währungseinheit	*monetary unit*	**Wichtigkeit**	*importance*
Wechsel		eine Sache von größter Wichtigkeit	*a matter of primary importance*
(Änderung)	*change*		
(Geldwechsel)	*exchange*		
(Zahlungsmittel)	*bill of exchange*		

Z

Zahlung	*payment*	**Ziel**	*goal, aim*
Abzahlungsgeschäft	*hire purchase*	(gesetztes)	*objective*
Anzahlung	*deposit, down-payment*	(Endziel)	*aim*
eine Anzahlung		(Reiseziel)	*destination*
von 30 %	*a deposit of 30 %*	(bildlich)	*target*
Ratenzahlung	*payment by instalments*	**Zielgruppe**	*target group*
Vorauszahlung	*payment in advance*		
		Zoll	
zeigen	*to show*	(Maß)	*inch, inches (")*
(ausweisen)	*to show*	(Abgabe)	*duty, customs duty*
(im Geschäft aus-		5 Zoll	*5 inches/ 5"*
stellen)	*to display*	Zölle	*tariffs*
(auf Messen ausstellen)	*to exhibit*	**Brückenzoll**	*toll*
(zeigen auf)	*to point to*	**Vorzugszölle**	*preferential tariffs*
Der Kontoauszug zeigt	*The statement of account*	**Zoll-** ...	*customs* ...,
einen Saldo von ...	*shows a balance of ...*	**Zollbehörde**	*customs authorities*
zu unseren Gunsten.	*in our favour.*	**Zolltarif, -satz, -gebühr**	*tariff, tariff rate*

Translate into English:

I   1 Sie verweigerten die Annahme der Sendung.
     2 Das Design der Maschine wurde geändert, und sie läuft jetzt besser.
     3 Diese Einfuhrbeschränkungen müssen abgeschafft werden.
     4 Der Auftrag kann nicht pünktlich ausgeführt werden.
     5 Es gibt genügend Arbeitskräfte in dieser Gegend.
     6 Die Angelegenheit wird sehr sorgfältig behandelt werden.
     7 Ihre Anfrage ist vertraulich behandelt worden.
     8 Unser Vertreter wird Sie innerhalb der nächsten 14 Tage besuchen.
     9 Es muß betont werden, daß wir keine Verantwortung in dieser Sache übernehmen.
   10 Die von Ihnen angebotene Druckmaschine ist teurer als die Ihrer Mitbewerber.

II 1 Alle diese Faktoren werden einen Einfluß auf die Wirtschaft unseres Landes haben.
     2 Einige unserer neuen Artikel wurden auf dem nordamerikanischen Markt eingeführt.
     3 Die Produktion solcher Artikel wird eingestellt werden.
     4 Die gelieferte Ware entspricht nicht Ihren Mustern.
     5 Wir werden alles tun, um Ihren Wünschen zu entsprechen.
     6 Die Regierung dieses Landes versucht ständig, den Lebensstandard der Armen zu erhöhen.
     7 Irrtümlich schickten wir Ihnen eine Rechnung über die Teile, die Ihnen kostenlos geliefert werden sollten.
     8 Der Verdächtige wurde von der Polizei befragt.
     9 In unserem Betrieb gibt es zur Zeit vier freie Stellen.
   10 Er führt sein Geschäft nun schon seit mehr als 20 Jahren mit großem Erfolg.

III 1 Wir sollten Maßnahmen zur Preissenkung ergreifen, um wettbewerbsfähiger zu sein.
    2 Wir sagen zu, die Ware in genau drei Tagen, d.h. am 1. Juni, zu verschicken.
    3 Der durchschnittliche Ertrag ist höchst zufriedenstellend.
    4 Der Preis versteht sich frei Grenze.
    5 Es besteht eine große Nachfrage nach unseren neu entwickelten Produkten überall in der westlichen Welt.
    6 Wir müssen Ihnen leider mitteilen, daß wir die Lieferzusage nicht einhalten können.
    7 Geschäfte beginnen oft mit einer Anfrage, die mündlich oder schriftlich gemacht wird.
    8 Diese Firma tätigt seit ungefähr 10 Jahren Geschäfte mit China.
    9 Moderne Maschinen sind mit elektronischen Überwachungssystemen ausgerüstet.
   10 Wir unterbreiteten Ihnen kürzlich ein Angebot über hochwertige Fernsehapparate.

IV 1 Gemäß unserer gültigen Preisliste beträgt der Preis dieses Artikels DM 50,–.
    2 Dieses Problem scheint unlösbar.
    3 Bis jetzt konnten wir keine Lösung dieses Problems finden.
    4 Er sammelt seit vielen Jahren Briefmarken.
    5 Dieses Reinigungsmittel ist ungefährlich.
    6 Alle eventuellen Nachteile sollten ebenfalls in Betracht gezogen werden.
    7 Sein Nettoeinkommen ist erstaunlich hoch.
    8 Bitte geben Sie uns Ihre offene Stellungnahme zu diesem Punkt.
    9 Beim Prüfen unserer offenen Rechnungen stellten wir fest, daß die Zahlung unserer Rechnung vom 22. Juli überfällig ist.
   10 Er wurde das Opfer einer Lawine/ein Opfer der Umstände.

V   1 Bitte schicken Sie die Schrauben per Paketpost.
    2 Unser Personalchef hat die unangenehme Aufgabe, ihm zu kündigen.
    3 Der Spediteur versäumte es, den notwendigen Schiffsraum zu buchen.
    4 Mit separater Post haben wir Ihnen Prospekte über unsere Produktpalette zugeschickt.
    5 Wir haben aus zuverlässiger Quelle erfahren, daß ihre Firma Konkurs angemeldet hat.
    6 Wir würden es begrüßen, wenn Sie die Rechnung sobald wie möglich begleichen könnten.
    7 Alle Klebstoffreste müssen sorgfältig entfernt werden.
    8 Aus Sicherheitsgründen müssen die Maschinen alle vier Wochen überprüft werden.
    9 Er sucht schon sein einer ganzen Zeit eine interessante Stelle.
   10 Das wird Probleme und Unannehmlichkeiten schaffen.

VI 1 Bei einer Störung wird die Maschine automatisch ausgeschaltet.
    2 Ihre Mitglieder kamen aus allen Bevölkerungsschichten.
    3 Die Maschinen arbeiten in drei Schichten, d.h. 24 Stunden am Tag.
    4 In den frühen 70er Jahren erlebten wir eine schwere Rezession.
    5 Durch Ausgleich von Angebot und Nachfrage kann der Preis stabil gehalten werden.
    6 Schließlich wurde der Vorschlag mit 20 zu 2 Stimmen angenommen.
    7 Handelsstreitigkeiten können durch Schiedsspruch beigelegt werden.
    8 Jede Industrie hat technische Begriffe, die oft nicht wörtlich übersetzt werden können.
    9 Um die Lage zu verbessern, sind tiefgreifende Änderungen erforderlich.
   10 Er war tief enttäuscht, daß er das Match verlor.

VII 1 Sie sucht eine Stelle, bei der sie Verantwortung übernehmen kann.
    2 In einem Sozialstaat erhalten Arbeitslose eine Arbeitslosenunterstützung.
    3 Wir werden vom 1. bis 22. Juni in Urlaub sein.

4 Vergessen Sie Ihre wichtige Verabredung um 11 Uhr in Köln nicht.
5 Wir würden uns freuen, Geschäftsbeziehungen mit Ihnen aufnehmen zu können.
6 Ein Vergleich ist die Beilegung von Handelsstreitigkeiten durch die Parteien selbst.
7 Unsere Verkäufer/unser Verkaufspersonal wird Sie gerne ausführlicher informieren.
8 Wir möchten Sie um eine zweimonatige Verlängerung unseres Kredits bitten.
9 Wenn Ihre Preise vernünftig sind, werden wir uns sicher einigen können.
10 Leider sind seine geschäftlichen und seine privaten Verpflichtungen sehr hoch.

VIII 1 Während der letzten beiden Monate verschlechterte sich die Sache.
2 Die Römischen Verträge wurden 1960 abgeschlossen.
3 Jede Lieferverzögerung wird uns große Unannehmlichkeiten bereiten.
4 Unsere Vorräte sind vollständig aufgebraucht.
5 Er hat wesentliche Fortschritte gemacht.
6 Die Verpflichtung zur Qualität ist unser wichtigstes Anliegen.
7 Die Zahlung muß durch unwiderrufliches Akkreditiv erfolgen.
8 In diesem Falle müssen wir auf Vorauszahlung bestehen.
9 Wir zeigten unsere neuesten Produkte auf der Leipziger Messe.
10 Ein Zoll ist 25,4 mm.

Fill in the right word:

1 **abziehen** *remove   withdraw   subtract   take out*

   To get the end result you must _____ the left-hand column from the right.

2 **Ansicht** *opinion   inspection   criticism   view*

   Please find enclosed a copy of our latest publication for your _____.

3 **besuchen** *visit   attend   call on   pay a visit*

   Each of our people has _____ a crash course in English.

4 **Druck** *printing   impression   pressure   compression*

   We do our best work under _____.

5 **einstellen** *discontinue   adjust   employ   suspend*

   Production of such articles will be _____.

6 **Fehler** *mistake   fault   error   defect*

   This was due to a _____ in the material.

7 **fördern** *promote   support   mine   further*

   _____ sales is his most important task.

8 **gewähren** *grant   concede   extend   advance*

   For orders exceeding 100 units we would be prepared to _____ you a quantity discount of 10 %.

9 **groß** *great huge vast substantial*

If your prices are competitive, we shall/will place a _____ order with you.

10 **Kiste** *case box crate chest*

Three_____ of Assam tea were shipped by MS Barbara yesterday.

11 **Kosten** *expenditure costs expense charges*

Any subsequent instruction of the operator will be at your _____.

12 **Leistung** *power capacity output achievement*

The _____ of this machine is 500 pieces per minute.

13 **Muster** *pattern sample model specimen*

Please send us a collection of _____ at your earliest convenience.

14 **Pause** *rest break pause interval*

At 10 a.m. we will have our coffee _____.

15 **Plan** *map plan schedule programme*

Make sure that the maintenance _____ is strictly observed/adhered to.

16 **prüfen** *check investigate test study*

We have carefully _____ your quotation dated January 3rd.

17 **Reihe** *row series range succession*

The _____ of reports on Africa is most interesting.

18 **schätzen** *appreciate assess estimate guess*

The value of his old car was _____ at approx. £ 1500.

19 **Schuld** *fault obligations guilt debts*

They have always met their _____ promptly.

20 **Spitze** *tip point peak lace*

The _____ load must not exceed 10,000 watt.

21 **Störung** *disturbance interruption interference trouble*

The electrician was sent for to find the _____.

22 **tragen** *carry bear support wear*

All risks and costs in connection with this order must be _____ by the buyer.

23 **verbessern** *improve modify correct amend*

Please send us your _____ invoice for the consignment shipped on May 4th.

24 **Wahl** *choice selection election alternative*

We have no _____ but to put the matter into the hands of our solicitors.

25 **Ziel** *goal aim objective target*

Foreign-language correspondents are the _____ group of this book.

2. Englische Wörter mit Doppel- und Mehrfachbedeutungen

Auch im Englischen gibt es viele Wörter mit Doppel- und Mehrfachbedeutungen. Man sollte sie nebeneinander gesehen haben, um überhaupt zu wissen, daß man beim Übersetzen aufpassen muß. Oft entstehen Sinnfehler, weil nicht beachtet wurde, daß ein bestimmtes Wort auch noch eine andere Bedeutung hat.
Die nachstehende Sammlung enthält Begriffe mit doppelter oder mehrfacher Bedeutung, die erfahrungsgemäß Schwierigkeiten bereiten.

accommodate [vb]
- beherbergen: *This region accommodates important industries. This hotel can only accommodate 35 guests.*
- entgegenkommen: *We shall accommodate you in this matter.*

act [n]
- Tat, Handlung: *a criminal act*
  Act of God – höhere Gewalt.
- Gesetz: *Act of Parliament*
  Stock Exchange Act – Börsengesetz
- (Theater)Akt

act [vb]
- handeln: *to act on one's own*

adjust [vb]
- einstellen: *The machine must be adjusted very carefully.*
- regulieren (von Reklamationen): *Please let us know how you intend to adjust this matter.*

adjustment [n]
- Einstellung: *The machine is out of adjustment.*
- Regulierung: *The adjustment we received on our insurance claim was larger than we had expected.*

admit [vb]
- zugeben: *He never admitted his mistake.*
- jemanden zu etwas zulassen: *The audience was admitted to the trial.*

advice [n]
- [kein Plural] Rat, Ratschläge: *She followed our advice.*
- Anzeige:
  advice of dispatch – Versandanzeige
  advice of remittance – Überweisungsanzeige

advise [vb]
- raten: *She advised this to be done.*
- ankündigen:
  an advised consignment – eine angekündigte Sendung

agent [n]
- Vertreter(in), Vermittler(in), Agent(in): *Please contact our agent.*
- (Putz)Mittel: *This cleaning agent removes all stains.*

34

allowance [n]
- eine regelmäßige Zahlung (oft vom Staat):
  maternity allowance – Mutterschaftsgeld
  child allowance – Kindergeld
- Nachlaß: *We shall grant you an allowance of 25 % if you are prepared to accept the goods partly damaged in transit.*

ask [vb]
- fragen (nach): *He asked the way to ...*
- bitten (um): *The child asked for a drink of water.*
  May I ask you a favour? – Darf ich Sie um einen Gefallen bitten?

Es gibt von *to ask (for)* in keiner der beiden Bedeutungen ein vom Verb abgeleitetes Substantiv. Frage – *question* Bitte – *request*

assemble [vb]
- versammeln (Menschen)
- zusammenbauen

assembly [n]
- Versammlung (Menschen):
  assembly hall – Sitzungssaal
- Zusammenbau: *The engine assembly must be completed before it can be fitted to the wing.*
  assembly line – Fließband

award [n]
- Belohnung, Auszeichnung, Prämie, Preis
- Entscheidung, Urteil:
  arbitrators's award – Schiedsspruch

award [vb]
- verleihen:
  He was awarded the prize.– Man verlieh ihm/Er bekam den Preis.

bank [n]
- Bank, Geldinstitut

Anstelle von *bank* kann man auch *bankers* sagen, wenn man sich auf *the senior level of the banking personnel* bezieht:*We will have have to consult our bankers before we consider taking over Buchan & Co. Ltd.*

- Ufer, Böschung: *On the banks of the river*

Merke: Eine Bank zum Sitzen ist "bench".

bill [n]
- Rechnung
- Gesetzesentwurf: *A bill becomes a law.*
- Wechsel, Kurzform für *bill of exchange*

board [n]
- Brett
- [großgeschrieben] Ausschuß:
  Board of Directors – Aufsichtsrat
  Tourist Board – Fremdenverkehrsamt

boring [adj]
boring [n]
- langweilig
- Ausbohren/Aufbohren eines Loches auf einen größeren Durchmesser

cancel [vb]
- absagen: *Flight No. 727 has been cancelled.*
- annullieren, stornieren, streichen: *The order was cancelled yesterday. Our subscription for this magazine will be cancelled.*
- ungültig machen, entwerten: *The cheque was cancelled.*

capital [n]
- Kapital:
    capital cost – Kapitalaufwand
    capital goods – Investitionsgüter
    capital stock – Kapital-/Stammaktien
    capital tax – Vermögenssteuer
- Hauptstadt: *Paris is the capital of France.*

capital [adj]
- Groß-, Haupt-:
    capital letter – Großbuchstabe

case [n]
- Fall:
    in the case of a – im Falle eines (einer)
    in any case – in jedem/auf jeden Fall
- Kiste:
    case markings – Kistenmarkierungen

Merke: Lattenkiste – *crate*   Teekiste – *chest*

cast [vb]
- werfen
- gießen:
    cast iron – Gußeisen

character [n]
- Charakter
- Buchstabe, Zeichen, Kenn-/Merkzeichen
- Original, besonderer Typ: *He is a character.*

characteristic [n]
- bezeichnendes Merkmal, technisches Leistungsmerkmal
characteristic [adj]
- *(of)* bezeichnend für

check [n]
- [US für *cheque*] Scheck
- [US für *bill*] Rechnung
check [vb]
- prüfen:
    to check in/out – sich an-/abmelden

China/china [n]
- China
- Porzellan:
    Dresden china – Meißner Porzellan

aber: *Delft ware* – Delfter Porzellan

collection [n]
- Sammlung
- Kollektion:
    sample collection – Musterkollektion
- Einzug von Geld:
    collection agency – Inkassobüro
    collection letter – Zahlungsaufforderung

	- Abholen von Waren: *The collection of the goods will be handled by our forwarding agents.* – Die Waren werden von unserem Spediteur abgeholt (werden).
column [n]	- Säule: *Nelson's Column* - Spalte (in Zeitung/Buch): *There are two columns to a page.*
concern [vb]	- betreffen, von Wichtigkeit sein: *to whom it may concern* – an alle, die es angeht *concerning* – betreffend
concern [n]	- Geschäft, Firma: *a paying concern* – ein lohnendes Geschäft - [meist Plural] Sache, Angelegenheit
concerned [adj]	- besorgt: *to be concerned* – besorgt sein *She was concerned for her mother.* – Sie war um ihre Mutter besorgt. *I am concerned to hear...* – Ich mache mir Sorgen ...
concrete [n] **concrete** [adj]	- Beton, Steinmörtel - konkret, fest, massig, kompakt
constitution [n]	- (Staats)Verfassung - Körperbeschaffenheit, Konstitution
control [n]	- Prüfung, Aufsicht: *quality control* - Steuerung [technisch]: *controlling instruments*
control [vb]	- prüfen, beaufsichtigen, steuern: *to control oneself* – sich beherrschen
course [n]	- Lauf, Ablauf: *in the course of* – im Laufe von *We shall inform you in due course.* – Wir werden Sie zu gegebener Zeit informieren. - Kurs, Lehrgang, Kursus: *Another course will be held next week.* – Ein weiterer Kurs wird nächste Woche stattfinden.
cover [n]	- Deckel, Abdeckung - (Buch)umschlag, Einband: *under separate cover* – mit getrennter Post
cover [vb]	- bedecken, abdecken - (ab)decken [bildlich], einschließen, enthalten: *The insurance will be covered by us.* – Die Versicherung wird von uns gedeckt (werden). *Are you covered by insurance?* – Sind Sie versichert? *A quotation should cover the following items...* – Ein Angebot sollte die folgenden Einzelheiten enthalten... *a covering letter* – ein Begleitschreiben

crash [n]
- Krach
- Unfall, Zusammenstoß:
  crash landing – Bruchlandung
- Intensiv-: *crash course, crash diet*

customs [n pl]
- Sitten
  We were not familiar with their customs and habits.– Wir waren mit ihren Sitten und Gebräuchen nicht vertraut.
- Zoll-:
  customs authorities – Zollbehörden
  customs duty – Zoll(abgabe)
  customs clearance – Zollabfertigung

damage [vb]
damage [n]
- beschädigen: *The goods arrived damaged.*
- Schaden, Beschädigung, Nachteil:
  The damage was more important than we had expected. – Der Schaden war größer als wir erwartet hatten.
  to my damage – zu meinem Nachteil

damages [n pl]
- Schadensersatz:
  action for damages – Schadensersatzklage
  to claim damages – Schadensersatz fordern

die [vb]
die [n]
- sterben
- Form, Gußform, Matrize
- Würfel

drawer [n]
- Schublade
- Aussteller eines Wechsels

Merke: *drawee* – Bezogener, d.h. derjenige, der zahlt

- Zeichner(in)

duty [n]
- Pflicht: *It is my duty to assist him.*
- *(customs) duty* – Zoll: *We had to pay duty on the goods.*

Heavy duty (Abkürzung *HD*) steht für strapazierfähig, robust. Hochleistungs-: *HD oil for automobiles*

either [conj]
either [adj]
- *either ... or* – entweder ... oder
- jede(r) von zweien:
  with either party – mit jeder (der beiden) Parteien
  on either side – auf jeder Seite
  You can walk on either side of the road. – Du kannst auf jeder/ auf beiden Seiten der Straße gehen.
  You can put glue on either side. – Du kannst auf jeder Seite Klebstoff auftragen.

Aber: *There must be glue on both sides.* – Auf beiden Seiten muß Klebstoff sein.

either [pron]
- (irgend)einer (von zweien):
  Either of you can do it. – Jeder von Euch beiden kann es tun.

enclose [vb]
- beifügen:
  Please find enclosed our quarterly statement of account. – Beigefügt schicken wir Ihnen unseren vierteljährlichen Kontoauszug.
- einfriedigen, umzäunen:
  enclosed land – eingefriedetes Land

enclosure [n]
- Beilage, Einlage:
  an enclosure in a letter – eine Anlage zu einem Brief
- Einfriedigung, Umzäunung

even [adv]
- sogar, selbst
even [adj]
- gerade, eben, glatt, gleichförmig

exercise [vb]
- üben
- trainieren, sich Bewegung verschaffen
- ausüben: *to exercise control*
exercise [n]
- Übung

experience [n]
- Erfahrung:
  He gathered great/a lot of experience from his position as Marketing Manager. – Er sammelte eine Menge Erfahrung in seiner Position als Leiter der Marketing-Abteilung.
- Erlebnis:
  Our stay in London was a great experience. – Unser Aufenthalt in London war ein großes Erlebnis.

execute [vb]
- ausführen:
  to execute an order – einen Auftrag ausführen
- hinrichten

execution [n]
- Ausführung:
  to promise prompt and careful execution of an order – die schnelle und sorgfältige Ausführung eines Auftrages versprechen/zusagen
- Hinrichtung

extension [n]
- Verlängerung, Vergrößerung
- Aufschub, Stundungsfrist: *She asked for extension of her library pass.*
- Anbau: *They are building an extension to the hospital.*
- [Telefon] Nebenstelle, Apparat

fair [adj]
- gerecht, fair
- blond, hell
fair [adv]
- ziemlich, leidlich: *fairly good*
fair [n]
- Messe, Jahrmarkt: *Leipzig Fair, Hanover Fair, Book Fair*

fine [adj]	- schön, gut: *I feel fine.*
fine [n]	- Bußgeld, Geldbuße, Strafe: *She had to pay a fine for speeding.*
fine [vb]	- Bußgeld verhängen: *He was fined £20 for speeding.*
firm [n]	- Firma: *This firm has specialized in building electronic parts.* – Diese Firma hat sich auf den Bau von Elektronikteilen spezialisiert.
firm [adj]	- fest: *to submit a firm offer* – ein verbindliches Angebot unterbreiten
form [n]	- Form, Gestalt - Formular, Vordruck: *business forms* – Geschäftsformulare
form [vb]	- formen

Bei einer Übersetzung vom Englischen ins Deutsche unterlief einer Sekretärin der folgende Fehler. Statt mit *Geschäftspapiere* über-setzte sie *business forms* ohne nachzudenken mit *der Beruf formt*.

interest [n]	- Interesse - Zinsen: *to earn/bear interest* – Zinsen bringen *interest-bearing* – zinsbringend *rate of interest* – Zinssatz - Anteil: *She has an interest in her brother's company.* – Sie hat Anteile an der Firma ihres Bruders.
issue [n]	- Ausgabe (einer Zeitung) - Ausstellung (von Paß, Aktie) - Frage, Problem: *Energy is a crucial issue.* – Die Energieversorgung ist eine entscheidende Frage.
issue [vb]	- herausgeben, herausgeben, ausstellen: *to issue a draft* – eine Tratte/einen Wechsel ausstellen *to issue coins/stamps* – Münzen/Briefmarken herausgeben
jam [n]	- Marmelade, Konfitüre - Störung, Stockung, Stau: *We got caught in a traffic jam.* – Wir steckten in einem Verkehrsstau.
jam [vb]	- fest-, einklemmen, quetschen: *The machine is jammed.* – Die Maschine arbeitet nicht. *He got his hand jammed.* – Er quetschte sich die Hand. - blockieren, sich drängen: *The square was jammed with people.* - [Radio, Sender] stören: *jamming station* – Störsender
key [n]	- Schlüssel: *keyword* – Schlüsselwort

	- Taste: *keyboard* – Bedienpult, Tastatur, Klaviatur
kind [n]	- Art: *all kinds of things* – alle möglichen Dinge
kind [adj]	- freundlich, gütig: *Would you be so kind as to help us? Kindly help us.* – Wären Sie bitte so freundlich, uns zu helfen?
last [adj]	- der, die, das letzte: *the last of the group* – der letzte der Gruppe Aber: *the latest (most recent) news* – die letzten (neuesten) Nachrichten
last [vb]	- dauern: *The meeting lasted two hours.* – Das Treffen dauerte zwei Stunden. *It will last me a week.* – Es wird mir eine Woche reichen. *lasting effect* – Dauerwirkung
late [adj]	- spät: *to be late* – zu spät kommen - (kürzlich) verstorben: *the late Mr. Smith*
line [n]	- Linie - Zeile: *We will write a few lines.* – Wir werden einige Zeilen schreiben. - Leine - Reihe, Schlange: *a long line of people* - Eisenbahnstrecke: *The line between Hamburg and Cologne* - Branche: *He has been working in this line for 10 years/since 1980.* – Er arbeitet seit 10 Jahren/seit 1980 in dieser Branche. - Gesellschaft: *an airline* – eine Fluggesellschaft
lock [vb]	- verschließen, sperren, verriegeln: *locking device* – Verriegelungseinrichtung
lock [n]	- Haarlocke - Verschluß, Verriegelung, Schloß: *under lock and key* – unter Verschluß *deadlock* – vollständige Stockung *They simply could not agree and so the meeting ended in deadlock.* – Sie konnten sich einfach nicht einigen, und deshalb endete das Treffen in einer Sackgasse. *locksmith* – Schlosser(in)
match [n]	- Wettkampf - Streichholz - das Passende, Ebenbürtige:

match [vb]	*an uneven match* – ein ungleiches Paar *matchless* – unvergleichlich, beispiellos *to be a match for a person* – jemandem gewachsen sein - zueinander passen: *The shirt and the trousers didn't match.* – Hemd und Hose paßten nicht zueinander. - gleichkommen: *Nobody can match her in accounting skills.* – Keiner ist in Buchführung so gut wie sie.
mind [vb]	- etwas dagegen haben: *Do you mind me/my opening the window?* – Haben Sie etwas dagegen, wenn ich das Fenster öffne? - aufpassen, beachten: *Mind the step!* – Vorsicht Stufe! - aufpassen auf: *She is minding the neighbour's children.* – Sie paßt auf die Kinder der Nachbarin auf.
mind [n]	- Erinnerung, Gedächtnis: *to bear in mind* – behalten, nicht vergessen *to have something in mind* – eine Idee haben, an etwas denken *to make up one's mind* – sich entschließen
minute [n] **minute** [adj]	- Minute - winzig, geringfügig, sehr genau
	Beachten Sie die Aussprache maɪˈnjuːt.
minutes [n pl]	- Minuten - Protokoll: *Who is taking the minutes?* – Wer schreibt Protokoll?
motion [n]	- Bewegung: *time-and-motion study* – Arbeitsstudie - Antrag: *to put forward a motion* – einen Antrag stellen *to grant a motion* – einem Antrag stattgeben
move [vb]	- bewegen - umziehen - beantragen: *to move an amendment to the motion* – einen Abänderungsantrag stellen
move [n]	- Schritt, Maßnahme: *a clever move* – ein geschickter Zug *to make the first move* – den ersten Schritt machen - Umzug
novel [n]	- Roman: *novelist* – Romanschriftsteller
novel [adj] **novelty** [n]	- neuartig: - Neuheit, etwas Neues:

Only one of our exhibits is a novelty. – Nur eines unserer Ausstellungsstücke ist eine Neuheit.

pension [n]
- Altersruhegeld, Pension:
  old-age pension – Rente, Pension
- [selten] Pension, Fremdenheim, Pensionat

perform [vb]
- vollbringen, leisten
- erfüllen:
  to perform a contract – einen Vertrag erfüllen

performance [n]
- (Theater)Vorstellung
- Leistung:
  a high-performance machine – eine Hochleistungsmaschine

pilot [n]
pilot [attr]
- Flugzeugführer(in), Pilot(in)
- Versuchs-:
  pilot plant – Versuchsanlage
  pilot project – Pilotprojekt

present [n]
present [vb]
- Geschenk
- vorlegen, präsentieren:
  to present a bill of exchange – einen Wechsel vorlegen

present [adj]
- anwesend:
  in the presence of – in Anwesenheit von

principal [n]
- Chef(in), Prinzipal, Hauptperson, Vorsteher(in)
- Auftraggeber(in) :
  The principal-agent relationship should be good. – Die Beziehungen zwischen Auftraggeber und Vertreter sollten gut sein.

principal [adj]
- hauptsächlich, führend:
  the principal debtor – der Hauptschuldner

rent [n]
- monatliche Miete:
  Rent Restriction Act – Mieterschutzgesetz
  rent control – Mietpreisbindung
- Riß, Spalte, [bildlich] Spaltung

rent [vb]
- mieten:
  Rent a car! – Autos zu vermieten! Mieten Sie ein Auto!

rest [n]
- Ruhe, Rast:
  a three days' rest – eine dreitägige Pause
  to take a rest – sich ausruhen
- Rest(menge):
  Most of the group are going to the Stock Exchange, I do not know what the rest will do. – Die meisten der Gruppe gehen zur Börse, ich weiß nicht, was der Rest tun wird.

rest [vb]
- ruhen:
  to let a matter rest – eine Sache auf sich beruhen lassen

realize [vb]	- realisieren, verwirklichen: *to realize a plan* - verstehen, begreifen: *they realized more and more that ...* – sie begriffen immer mehr, daß ...
save [vb]	- retten: *SOS - Save our ships/souls.* – Internationales Seenotzeichen - sparen: *to save money, to save time, time-saving*
since [prep]	- seit: *(Ever) since the manager started paying piece rates, the output has slowly increased.* – Seit der Geschäftsführer die Zahlung von Akkordsätzen eingeführt hat, steigt die Produktion langsam.

> Merke: *He has been learning English since 1980* [Zeitpunkt, seit wann]. *He has been learning English for 10 years* [Zeitraum, wie lange].

since [conj]	- seitdem: *I have not seen him since.* – Seitdem habe ich ihn nicht gesehen. - da: *Since (as) he was busy, he could not come to the meeting.*
security [n] **securities** [n pl]	- Sicherheit - Effekten, Wertpapiere
sentence [n] **sentence** [vb]	- Satz - Urteil, Rechtsspruch: *sentence of confinement* – Arreststrafe - verurteilen: *to be sentenced to death* – zum Tode verurteilt werden
settle [vb]	- sich niederlassen, siedeln - erledigen: *to settle an invoice* – eine Rechnung begleichen *to settle a matter* – eine Angelegenheit erledigen/in Ordnung bringen
settlement [n]	- Niederlassung, Siedlung: *the first settlements in North America* - Erledigung: *in settlement of your invoice* – zum Ausgleich/in Erledigung Ihrer Rechnung
shift [vb] **shift** [n]	- verschieben, verrücken, versetzen, [technisch] schalten - Veränderung, Verschiebung - Schicht: *day shift, night shift*
sleeve [n]	- Ärmel: *a shirt with short sleeves* - Hülle: *record sleeve* – Schallplattenhülle - [technisch] Büchse
some [adj]	- [nicht zählbar] etwas: *some sugar* - [zählbar] einige: *some books*

some [adv]   - ungefähr: *There were some 100 people there.*

sound [n]   - Laut, Ton, Klang
sound [adj]   - gesund, fundiert:
                             a sound judgement – eine fundierte Beurteilung
                             a sound company – eine sichere, solide Firma
                             sound health – gute Gesundheit

spring [n]   - Frühling
                             - Quelle, Brunnen, Ursprung
                             - [technisch] Feder
spring/springiness [n]   - Elastizität, Sprungkraft
spring [vb]   - springen:
                             to spring back – zurückspringen
                             to spring up – aufspringen, aufkommen, entstehen
                             - zersprengen, quellen

statement [n]   - Behauptung
                             - Kontoauszug:
                             Please find enclosed our quarterly statement of account showing a balance of ... in our favour. – Beiliegend übersenden wir Ihnen unseren vierteljährlichen Kontoauszug, der einen Saldo von ... zu unseren Gunsten ausweist.

still [adv]   - noch
still [adj]   - still: *the machine stands still*
                             during a standstill of the machine – während eines Stillstandes der Maschine

> aber: er ist still (schweigsam) – *he is silent*
>   er ist still (ruhig) – *he is quiet*
>   die See liegt still – *the sea is calm*

stock [n]   - Lager von Waren, Vorrat: *We are sorry to inform you that the goods are no longer in stock.*
                             - *(shares)* Aktien:
                             stock market – Aktienmarkt
                             stock corporations [US] – Kapitalgesellschaften
                             stockholder [US] – Effekteninhaber(in), Aktionär(in)
                             Stock Exchange – Börse
                             stock jobber/broker – Börsenmakler(in)

story [n]   - Geschichte, Novelle
                             - [US] Etage, Stockwerk [GB: *storey*]

subject [n]   - Subjekt: *the subject of a sentence*
                             - Thema: *the subject of a discussion*
                             - Betreff: *the subject of a letter*
                             - Untergebene(r): *the subject of a monarch*
                             - Unterrichtsfach: *the various subjects at school*

subject [adj]
- *to be subject to*
  The prices are subject to alterations. – Preisänderungen vorbehalten.
  Subject to alterations in price without notice – Preisänderungen ohne vorherige Ankündigung.
  These parts are subject to increased wear. – Diese Teile unterliegen einem erhöhten Verschleiß.

succeed [vb]
- gelingen:
  I succeeded in improving my English. – Es gelang mir, mein Englisch zu verbessern.
- folgen, nachfolgen:
  He succeeded her to the throne. – Er war ihr Thronnachfolger.

survey [n]
- Übersicht:
  The enclosed brochure is to give you a survey on our manufacturing programme. – Der beigefügte Prospekt soll Ihnen einen Überblick über unser Fabrikationsprogramm geben.
- Besichtigung, Schätzung, Prüfung:
  survey report – Havariezertifikat
  surveyor – Havariekommissar(in), Landvermesser(in), Sachverständige(r)

table [n]
- Tisch
- Tabelle

tender [adj]
- zärtlich, besorgt

tender [n]
- Angebot, Submissionsangebot:
  A tender is a quotation made in response to an invitation to tender. – Ein Submissionsangebot ist ein Angebot, das auf eine Ausschreibung hin gemacht wird.

tender [vb]
- anbieten, beantragen:
  to tender one's resignation – seine Entlassung einreichen/beantragen

term [n]
- Ausdruck, Fachausdruck
- Semester an einer britischen Universität oder Schule

terms [n pl]
- Bedingungen:
  terms of payment and delivery – Lieferungs- und Zahlungsbedingungen
  We cannot accept these terms. – Wir können diese Bedingungen nicht annehmen.
  to come to terms – sich (nach Verhandlungen) einig werden

title [n]
- Titel: *This book has an interesting title.*
- Anspruch (auf Eigentum oder Besitz):
  reservation of property or title – Eigentumsvorbehalt

trial [n]
- Versuch, Probe:
  trial order – Probeauftrag
- gerichtliches Verfahren

try [vb] - versuchen, ausprobieren
 - einen Fall juristisch untersuchen, jemanden vor Gericht bringen

while [n] - Weile:
 for a while – eine Zeitlang
while [conj] - während: *While we were working, he was reading.*

Fill in the missing words:

1. The amount according to the enclosed _____ of remittance was remitted to your account with the Deutsche Bank, Munich, on June 6th.
2. Last year, he was _____ the Nobel Prize.
3. The matter has been given to a _____ agency that will collect the money.
4. We are sorry that we must claim _____ due to the delayed delivery of the goods ordered for arrival on November 1st.
5. We will place a substantial order with you if you can promise a prompt and careful _____.
6. Our children's education is a crucial _____.
7. The amount is payable on _____ of the bill of exchange.
8. After a three hours' _____ they continued their excursion.
9. Please find enclosed a cheque in _____ of our invoice of August 23rd 1990.
10. The enclosed _____ of account shows a balance of £ 525 in our favour.
11. Your competitors' _____ of delivery and payment are more favourable than yours.
12. We should like to check the quality of your rubber gloves and, therefore, place a _____ order for 3 pairs, article No. 50, with you.

Übersetzen Sie ins Deutsche:

1. We are ready/prepared to accommodate you in this matter.
2. Please let us know by return/as soon as possible/at your earliest convenience, how you intend to adjust this matter.
3. No audience was admitted to the trial.
4. If you are prepared to keep/accept the goods, we shall/will grant you an allowance of 10%.
5. He told us that assembly line work was very monotonous.
6. The bill of exchange was presented to our bankers yesterday.
7. The Board of Directors came to the conclusion that a diversification of the delivery programme was advisable.
8. Do you sell capital goods or consumer goods?
9. All cases to overseas countries will have to be marked according to the customers' instructions.
10. We understand that you will inform us in more detail in due course.
11. The customs authorities required an exact description of the articles you delivered.
12. The drawee was not in a position to honour the bill of exchange at maturity.
13. It is absolutely necessary to exercise regular control.
14. The Hanover Fair is one of the most important exhibitions in the world.
15. Please submit a firm offer for the spare parts specified on the enclosed list.
16. Within the last months the rate of interest has risen slightly.
17. The buttons and keys on the control board are black and red.
18. After working/having worked in this trade/line for 40 years, he retired.
19. We must take appropriate measures/steps to settle the matter to our customers' entire satisfaction.
20. After a long debate they made up their minds and decided to go ahead with the project.
21. The minutes of the meeting contain many interesting details.
22. They put forward a motion which was then granted.
23. This novel is by Simmel.
24. Her old-age pension is lower than she had expected.
25. At this year's Leipzig Fair we exhibited a high-performance machine for manufacturing serviettes.
26. The agent works on behalf of his principal.
27. Rent a car and visit the most beautiful areas of our country.
28. By using this new machine you will save time and money.
29. He has been playing tennis for many years and is now one of the most successful players of our club.
30. The murderer of the old lady was sentenced to death.
31. Clean the machine after every shift!
32. There were some 200 young people who attended/took the different language courses.
33. This is a sound company which enjoys an excellent reputation in its field.
34. We are pleased to place an order for 100 springs No. 251 601 with you.
35. We regret having to tell you that the parts you ordered on January 2nd are not available/in stock.
36. Our visit to the Stock Exchange was a great experience.
37. The spare parts catalogue contains the components which are subject to increased wear.
38. We succeeded in finding some new markets for our products.
39. Please send us a leaflet/brochure giving a survey of your delivery program(me).
40. For a while she was the best player of our group.

3. Der richtige Umgang mit Fremdwörtern

Schwerwiegende Sinnfehler, auch lustige Verwechslungen entstehen, weil Fremdwörter nicht übersetzt, sondern einfach übernommen werden. Es ist so bequem, ein Fremdwort (dessen Bedeutung manchmal gar nicht so recht verstanden wird) einfach in die jeweils andere Sprache zu übertragen.

Es ist sehr wichtig zu wissen, daß gewisse Wörter ihre Bedeutung ändern, wenn sie in einer anderen Sprache angewendet werden.

Es sei also wirklich ausdrücklich davor gewarnt, Fremdwörter einfach zu übernehmen und anzunehmen, daß man sich um dieses Wort keine weiteren Gedanken machen müsse.

Das ist übrigens in allen Sprachen so. Es gibt da im Französischen so ein einleuchtendes Beispiel: Eine Volksschullehrerin nennt man in Frankreich auch *maîtresse*!

Natürlich gibt es auch viele Fremdwörter, die in die jeweils andere Sprache übernommen werden können, z.B. *budget,* wenn es sich um den Etat, (Staats)Haushalt handelt, oder *traditional*. Andere Fremdwörter müssen in bestimmten Bereichen sogar übernommen werden. Denken wir an *frequency*, das in der Elektrik mit „Frequenz" übersetzt werden muß, also nicht mit Häufigkeit.

Nachstehend die erfahrungsgemäß am häufigsten gemachten Fehler, wobei die Ungenauigkeit oder falsche Übersetzung daher kommen kann, daß das Fremdwort einfach aus dem Englischen übernommen wurde (siehe Beispiel *construction*) oder aber ein in der deutschen Sprache übliches Fremdwort lediglich übertragen wurde (siehe Beispiel „Branche").

| Vorsicht bei folgenden **englischen** Begriffen: |

actual(ly) *Actual* mit aktuell zu übersetzen, wäre einfach aber falsch. *Actual(ly)* bedeutet tatsächlich, eigentlich:
What was her actual decision?
What do you actually want me to do?
→ aktuell

agent *Agent* entspricht nur manchmal dem deutschen Agent. Die verschiedenen Bedeutungen sind:
- Handelsvertreter(in):
  shipping/forwarding agents – Spediteure
- Mittel:
  clean(s)ing agents – Reinigungsmittel
- Agent, Spion

career Im Deutschen bedeutet Karriere meist ein schnelles (berufliches) Fortkommen. Im Englischen steht *career* für Laufbahn im allgemeinen:
He entered upon a career in the diplomatic service once the war came to an end.
Her business career was briefly interrupted for two years when she started a family.
His entire professional career has been spent in the packaging industry.

caution	- Vorsicht, Warnung, Achtung: *The major advised me to proceed with extreme caution once I had crossed into enemy territory.* *The label on the medicine bottle read* CAUTION - KEEP OUT OF REACH OF CHILDREN. - Kaution, aber nur durch den Zusatz von *money*: *Before we could move into our new flat we had to pay 3 months' caution money.*
commission	- Provision (nicht Kommission): *The agent acts on commission basis.* *We shall grant you a 10 % commission on all orders placed in your sales territory.* Merke: Kommissionslager (Konsignationslager) – *consignment stock* - Auftrag: *My first major commission as an architect was to design a shopping mall in the centre of Liverpool.* - Ausschuß, Kommission: *After the sinking of the Titanic, a commission was appointed to investigate why the ship went down so quickly.*
confection	- Konfekt, Zuckerwerk: *confectionery industry* – Süßwarenindustrie - modischer Artikel (Damenbekleidung)
consequently	Dieses Wort hat nichts mit dem deutschen → konsequent zu tun; es heißt: - folglich, infolgedessen.
construction	Dieses Wort hat nicht den Sinn des deutschen Wortes → Konstruktion, wie z.B. in Konstruktionsabteilung und Konstruktionsbüro, wo etwas entwickelt bzw. entworfen wird, sondern: - Errichten, Bauen (von Gebäuden, Straßen, Brücken, Maschinen): *The construction of the Channel Tunnel is a multi-million pound project.* *The machine designed by our engineering department* (Konstruktionsabteilung) *or the design office* (Konstruktionsbüro) *is now under construction* (in Bau).
dealer	Nicht jeder *dealer* ist im Englischen ein Rauschgifthändler! - Händler(in), Vertragshändler(in): *Repair work on these tape recorders is best carried out by the authorized dealer.* *deal* – Handel; Geschäft, das getätigt wird *to deal in* – handeln mit (Waren) *to deal with* – sich beschäftigen mit - Rauschgifthändler(in)
decade	Im Deutschen verstehen wir unter Dekade zehn Tage. Nicht so im Englischen: - Jahrzehnt: *The last decade of this century began on 1st January 1990.* *I have known him for decades.* - Serie von zehn

discretion	- Freiheit, Ermessen: *at your discretion* – nach Ihrem Belieben, Gutdünken, Ermessen *It is within your discretion to decide in this way.* – Es steht Ihnen frei, die Entscheidung in dieser Richtung zu treffen. - Diskretion, Verschwiegenheit, vertrauliche Behandlung: *This information should be used with discretion.*
engineer	Der deutsche Ingenieur hat einen Titel erworben, der englische *engineer* ist ein Techniker im allgemeinen: *Our engineers will certainly be in a position to assist you in finding the best solution to this problem.* *engineering* – Technik, Maschinenbaukunst *engineering department* – technische Abteilung *engineering facilities* – technische Einrichtungen *engineering process* – technisches Verfahren *engineering science* – technische Wissenschaft
eventual(ly)	Vorsicht bei diesem Wort; es bedeutet nicht eventuell (möglicherweise) sondern, schließlich, endlich: *The eventual success of this transaction will be decisive.* *She will get accustomed to it eventually.* *eventuality* – (möglicher) Fall, Eventualität
fatal(ly)	*Fatal* bedeutet im Englischen mehr als im Deutschen: - schicksalsmäßig, unvermeidlich, Schicksals- - gefährlich, verhängnisvoll: *a fatal situation* - tödlich: *He was fatally wounded.*
invalid	Das englische Wort entspricht nur bedingt dem deutschen Wort → Invalide. Mit der Betonung ın'vælıd heißt es: - (rechts)ungültig - gegenstandlos, hinfällig
origin/original(ly)	Wenn diese Wörter auch die Bedeutung des deutschen ursprünglich haben, müssen sie in Fachbegriffen oft anders übersetzt werden: *original copy* – Erstausführung eines Schriftstücks *certificate of origin* – Ursprungszeugnis *country of origin* – Herkunftsland *national origin* – Staatsangehörigkeit
pamphlet	Pamphlet kann nicht einfach ins Deutsche übernommen werden, da es dort nur die Bedeutung von Flugschrift, meist Schmähschrift, abdeckt. Im Englischen kann es auch Broschüre bedeuten.
personal	*Personal* heißt nicht Personal sondern ist ein Adjektiv und heißt persönlich. Ein *personal data sheet* enthält die Angaben zur Person in einer Bewerbung. *personal estate* – bewegliches Vermögen *personal appearance* – äußerliches Erscheinungsbild

prospect

Prospect bedeutet nicht Prospekt oder Werbeschrift:
- Aussicht
- Kurzform von *prospective customer* – möglicher, zukünftiger Kunde

> Ein beliebter Fehler: *Please find enclosed our latest prospect* (anstelle von *prospectus, leaflet, brochure*)!

public

- Öffentlichkeit
- öffentlich:
  public transport – öffentliche Verkehrsmittel
  public relations – Öffentlichkeitsarbeit

> Aber: *public school* [England, Wales] – Privatschule, z.B. Eton
> *public school* [USA, Schottland] – Volksschule
> Die öffentliche Schule in England und Wales ist *state school*.

rate

Rate ist nicht das, was man im Deutschen oft darunter versteht, also der festgesetzte Betrag einer Ratenzahlung. → Rate. Das englische Wort *rate* steht meistens im Sinne von Quote, Satz:
unemployment rate – Arbeitslosenrate
exchange rate – Wechselkurs
discount rate – Diskontsatz
interest rate – Zinssatz
rate of dividend – Dividende

serious(ly)

Serious sieht dem deutschen Wort seriös ähnlich, bedeutet im Englischen aber ernsthaft, ernstlich:
a serious situation
He was seriously ill.
She seriously considered the proposition.

solid

- fest (nicht flüssig):
  solid fuel – fester Kraftstoff
  solid contents – Festgehalt
- massiv, Voll-:
  solid silver – Vollsilber
- [bildlich] kreditwürdig:
  sound and solid (creditworthy) – kreditwürdig und reell
- gediegen, solide

sympathetic

Sympathetic sieht wie sympathisch aus, es heißt aber in erster Linie einfühlend, mitfühlend, verständnisvoll, wohlwollend usw. Heute wird es jedoch bereits von vielen englischen Muttersprachlern wie das deutsche sympathisch verwendet.

tariff

Tariff heißt nicht in jedem Falle Tarif, es steht oft für Zoll:
tariff act – Zollgesetz
tariff union – Zollunion
preferential tariffs – Vorzugszölle
abolition of tariffs – Aufhebung der Zölle
Zu Begriffen, in denen *tariff* mit dem deutschen Tarif übereinstimmt, → Tarif.

tip	- Spitze - Trinkgeld: *to tip a waiter* – einem Kellner ein Trinkgeld geben - Tip, Ratschlag *Let me give you a tip: don't talk to the boss today about your salary, because he's in a terrible mood.* Tip, Wink, Fingerzeig übersetzt man mit *hint*.
vital(ly)	*Vital* ist zwar auch vital im deutschen Sinne, aber in der Hauptsache lebensnotwendig. *vital economic necessity* – wirtschaftliche Lebensnotwendigkeit *energy is a vital issue* – Energie, eine lebensnotwendige Frage

Never use words whose meaning you have not fully grasped!

Vorsicht bei folgenden **deutschen** Begriffen:

aktuell	Aktuell übersetzt man mit *current* – laufend, *present* – augenblicklich und *topical* – das, worüber man gerade spricht, aber auf keinen Fall mit *actual*.
Branche	Das deutsche Wort Branche ist nicht mit *branch* zu übersetzen: Textilbranche – *textile trade* Er arbeitet schon seit langem in dieser Branche. – *He has been working in this trade for a long time.* Werbung ist nicht unser Fach (wir arbeiten nicht in der Werbebranche). – *Advertising is not our line.* Merke: Zweigstelle (einer Bank) – *branch office (of a bank)*.
Dekade	→ *decade*
Diskretion	Wenn man in Auskunftsbriefen oder dergleichen um Diskretion bittet, wählt man meist Ausdrücke wie *to treat a piece of information as strictly confidential, to hold a piece of information in strict confidence, private and confidential* (auf einem vertraulichen Brief) aber auch: *This information should be used with discretion.*
fatal	Wollen Sie das deutsche fatal auf englisch wiedergeben, benutzen Sie Wörter wie *dreadful, disagreeable, annoying, bad* usw., also nicht → *fatal*. eine fatale Situation – *a nasty situation*
Fusion	*Fusion* bedeutet Verschmelzung im allgemeinen, aber nicht die Fusion, den Zusammenschluß zweier Firmen. Das ist *merger* und *amalgamation*.
Invalide	Nur selten spricht man von *invalid*, was ja mit anderer Betonung ungültig heißt. Invalide, Versehrter – *disabled person*

Invalidität – *disability, disablement*
Invalidenrente – *disability pension*

Investition Investition (Geldanlage) ist im Englischen *investment*.

Kaution Nicht *caution* – Vorsicht, sondern *caution money*.

Konjunktur Nicht *conjuncture* – Verbindung, Zusammentreffen von Umständen usw. Die wirtschaftliche Konjunktur ist *business cycle*.
konjunkturelle Entwicklung – *economic trend*
Trends – *trend of business, cyclical trends*
Konjunkturschwankungen – *cyclical fluctuations*
Hochkonjunktur – *boom*
Wirtschaftskrise, Baisse – *slump*

Konkurrenz Konkurrenz (Wettbewerb) ist *competition*. Das englische *concurrence* bedeutet Übereinstimmung, Zustimmung und *(of events)* Zusammentreffen (von Ereignissen).
We have to face keen competition.
Our prices are competitive.
We can offer at more favourable prices than our competitors.

konsequent/ konsequenterweise Diese Wörter kann man nicht mit *consequent(ly)* übersetzen; es muß *consistent (ly)* oder manchmal auch *strict(ly)* heißen. → *consequently*

Konstruktion → *construction*
Konstruktion – *design*
Konstruktionsbüro – *design office*
Konstrukteur – *designer, draughtsman*
In den folgenden Beispielen bezieht man sich auf die Bauweise:
Konstruktionsmerkmale – *constructional features*
Eisenkonstruktion – *iron construction*
Wenn es sich um die Konstruktion im Sinne von Aufbau handelt, ist dies *structure*.

Kultur Nicht in jedem Falle wird Kultur mit *culture* übersetzt. Einige Beispiele, um die Unterschiede herauszustellen:
Kultur, die man hat – *civilization*
Kultur haben – *to be civilized*
eine Seidenkultur – *a culture of silk*
eine kultivierte Sprache – *a cultured language*
Bodenkultur – *cultivation of soil*

Original Bedeutet dieses Wort ursprünglich, ist es übertragbar. Sagen wir im Deutschen aber: „Er ist ein Original.", so heißt das im Englischen: *"He is a character"*.

Personal Das Personal einer Firma ist *personnel* oder *staff*.
personal – persönlich
Personalabteilung – *personnel department*
Personalchef – *staff manager*

pro	Die lateinische Vorsilbe pro gibt es im Englischen in der im Deutschen üblichen Bedeutung nicht, das ist *per*. pro Jahr – *per year* pro Nacht – *per night* pro Person – *per person* *the price for a hotel room per person, per night* Prozent – *percent* Aber: zweimal pro/in der Woche – *twice a week* einmal pro/im Jahr – *once a year* dreimal pro/im Monat – *three times a month*
Prospekt	Prospekt ist nicht → *prospect* sondern *prospectus, leaflet, folder* und – besonders im Amerikanischen – *brochure*. *Please find enclosed our quotation together with a leaflet for the latest version of this machine.*
Provision	Die an einen Vertreter zu zahlende Provision ist im Englischen *commission*. *We shall grant you a commission of 10 %.* Das englische *provision* kommt von *to provide* und bedeutet Versorgung, Proviant.
Rate	Eine Rate, der festgesetzte Betrag einer Ratenzahlung, ist nicht *rate* sondern *instalment*. Steuerrate – *tax instalment* Rate im Sinne von Quote, Satz, kann aber übernommen werden. Arbeitslosenrate – *unemployment rate*
Reklamation	Die Reklamation, Beschwerde, Mängelrüge, von der man im kaufmännischen Englisch spricht, ist *complaint* (von *to complain of*). Ihre Reklamation wird sehr sorgfältig geprüft werden. – *Your complaint will be checked very carefully.* Im Sinne von Reklamation, Protest ist *reclamation* richtig.
seriös	Mit seriös meinen wir im Deutschen zuverlässig, verantwortungsbewußt, und so wird es auch übersetzt, nämlich mit *reliable, responsible*. *They are reliable business partners.* → *serious*
Tarif	Tarif kann nicht in jedem Falle mit *tariff* übersetzt werden. Übereinstimmend ist die Bedeutung z.B. in Tarif bei Eisenbahn, Luftfracht. Zoll – *tariff* Zolltarif – *customs tariff* Vorzugszoll – *preferential tariff* Die Tarifverhandlungen zwischen Arbeitgebern und Arbeitnehmern zur Festsetzung neuer tariflicher Löhne werden mit *collective bargaining* übersetzt.
Tip	Ein Tip im Sinne von Wink, Fingerzeig ist ein *hint*.

Benutzen Sie nie ein Wort, dessen Bedeutung Sie nicht genau kennen!

Translate into English:

1. Unsere Spedition wird für die Abholung der Ware am 21. Januar in Ihrer Fabrik sorgen.
2. Bevor wir ihm unsere Vertretung übertragen, müssen wir darauf bestehen, daß er eine Kaution zahlt.
3. Unsere Vertretungen erhalten eine Provision von 10 % auf alle getätigten Verkäufe.
4. Wir bestätigen, daß die von Ihnen bestellte Maschine in Bau ist.
5. Sie handeln seit über 30 Jahren mit Autos und haben einen bemerkenswerten Erfolg.
6. Vor drei Tagen hatte er einen Unfall und wurde tödlich verletzt.
7. Lieferungen/Sendungen in bestimmte Länder muß ein Ursprungszeugnis beigelegt werden.
8. Im Augenblick sind die Geschäftsaussichten außerordentlich gut.
9. Die Arbeitslosenrate in Großbritannien ist höher als die in Deutschland.
10. In den letzten drei Monaten ist der Zinssatz beträchtlich gefallen.
11. Er soll ernstlich krank sein.
12. Man sagt, daß diese Firma gesund und kreditwürdig ist.
13. Die Aufhebung der Zölle ist eine der Maßnahmen zur Förderung des Handels.
14. Sie gab dem Kellner ein großzügiges Trinkgeld.
15. Wir müssen darauf bestehen, daß Sie unsere Auskunft vertraulich behandeln.
16. Der Zusammenschluß dieser beiden Firmen war eine gute Entscheidung.
17. Ab 1. Januar nächsten Jahres wird seine Invalidenrente um 2½ % erhöht werden.
18. Die Konstruktionsabteilung ist überlastet und macht seit Monaten Überstunden.
19. Dieser Junge ist ein echtes Original.
20. Die Personalchefin ist die Leiterin der Personalabteilung.
21. Wir besuchen unsere Kunden zweimal im Jahr, um alle offenen Fragen zu besprechen.
22. Eine Mängelrüge muß sehr vorsichtig behandelt werden, so daß die betreffenden Kunden wieder zufriedengestellt sind.

Was ist falsch?

1. Since we have to face keen concurrence, we are forced to lower our prices. For this reason, your provision will have to be reduced to 5% instead of the usual 10%.

   _____   _____

2. Your reclamations have been brought to my attention. _____

3. The construction department will send you the plans for the new machine.

   _____

4. The company is successful because they apply new methods consequently. _____

5. During the last three years, there has been a considerable decline in business in the textile branch, but now things are changing for the better. _____

6. For your information we are enclosing prospects on our range of products. _____

7. They pay their new furniture in monthly rates. _____

8. The fusion of the airlines caused hectic trading on the stock exchange. _____

4. Wortgruppen

Wenn Sie diese Wortgruppen lernen, sollten Sie sich dabei vor allem über die kleinen Unterschiede in der Schreibweise klarwerden. Die Aufstellung enthält auch einige Begriffe, die der Wortgruppe nach nicht zueinander gehören, aber denselben Stamm haben (z.B. *custom, customs*).
Es wird hier darauf verzichtet, alle Zusammensetzungen aufzuführen. Die nachfolgende Aufstellung beinhaltet nur die Basiswörter und hier und da einen für Wirtschafts- und Korrespondenz-Englisch besonders wichtigen Begriff. Zusammensetzungen können dann in den meisten Fällen sehr leicht durchgeführt werden.
Am Ende der Einträge wird vielfach auch auf Gegensätze hingewiesen, die durch Hinzufügung einer Vorsilbe oder einer Nachsilbe gebildet werden.
Wenn Sie das Gegenteil eines Wortes suchen, probieren Sie es doch einmal mit den Vorsilben *de, dis, il, im, in, irr, mis, non* und *un* bzw. mit der Nachsilbe *less*.
Viele Schwierigkeiten gibt es bei den Wörtern, die den Gegensatz mit den Vorsilben *in* oder *un* ausdrücken. Es soll einmal jemand den Tip gegeben haben, in diesen Fällen möglichst undeutlich zu sprechen, damit die Unsicherheit nicht auffiele. Aber schließlich kann man ja nicht undeutlich schreiben! Da muß man sich schon entscheiden. Besser noch, man weiß es einfach.

a

adequacy	- Angemessenheit, Zulänglichkeit	*dis*advantage	- Nachteil
adequate (to)	- angemessen, entsprechend, ausreichend	*dis*advantageous	- unvorteilhaft
		to advertise	- Werbung machen für
*in*adequate	- unangemessen, ungenügend, unzureichend		- inserieren, annoncieren
		advertisement	- Anzeige, Werbung
to adjust	- einstellen, verstellen	advertiser	- Inserent(in)
	- abstimmen, angleichen, anpassen	advertising	- Werbung, Reklame
		advertising agency	- Werbeagentur
to adjust oneself to	- sich einer Sache anpassen, sich auf etwas einstellen	advice	- Benachrichtigung, Avis
			- Mitteilung, Meldung, Ratschlag
adjustability	- Verstellbarkeit, Anpassungsfähigkeit	advisable	- zweckmäßig, ratsam
adjustable	- verstellbar	to advise	- benachrichtigen
adjuster	- Einsteller		- raten
adjustment	- Einstellung, Verstellung, Anpassung	advisor, adviser	- Berater(in)
		advisory	- beratend
	- Beilegung, Schlichtung, Regulierung	to analyse	- analysieren, untersuchen
non-adjustable	- nicht verstellbar	analysis	- Analyse, Untersuchung
advantage	- Vorteil	analyst	- Analytiker(in)
advantageous(ly)	- vorteilhaft	analytic, analytical(ly)	- analytisch

annual(ly)	- jährlich	approval	- Zustimmung
annual	- Jahrbuch, Jahresalbum	to approve	- zustimmen
annualization	- Umrechnung auf Jahresbasis	*dis*approval	- Mißbilligung
to annualize	- auf Jahresbasis berechnen	to assert	- behaupten
		assertion	- Behauptung
annuity	- Jahreseinkommen	assertive(ly)	- bestimmt
	- Lebensrente	assertiveness	- Bestimmtheit
	- Annuität (Wertpapier)		
		to assume	- vermuten, annehmen
apparent	- sichtbar, offenbar	assumption	- Annahme, Mutmaßung
apparently	- scheinbar		
to appear	- erscheinen, sich zeigen	author	- Autor(in), Verfasser(in), Schriftsteller(in)
appearance	- Erscheinen, Erscheinung		
to *dis*appear	- verschwinden	authoritarian [adj]	- autoritär
*non*appearance	- Nichterscheinen	authoritarian [n]	- autoritärer Mensch
		authoritative	- bestimmt, entschieden
to apply	- anwenden, verwenden		- zuverlässig, maß-
	- verwenden, auftragen		gebend
to apply for	- sich bewerben um, beantragen	authoritatively	- mit Autorität, bestimmt, maßgeblich
applicability	- Anwendbarkeit, Eignung	authority	- Autorität
applicable	- anwendbar		- Befugnis
applicant	- Bewerber(in)		- Behörde
application	- Anwendung, Ver- wendung	authorization	- Genehmigung, Er- mächtigung
	- Bewerbung, Antrag	to authorize	- autorisieren, ermäch- tigen
applicator	- Applikator, Aufträger		
applied	- angewandt	to be authorized	- berechtigt sein
applied cost	- zugerechnete Kosten	authorship	- Autor-, Verfasserschaft
*in*applicable	- nicht anwendbar		- Schriftstellerberuf

b

belief	- Glaube, Überzeugung, Vertrauen	benefactor, -factress	- Gönner(in)
		beneficial	- vorteilhaft
believable	- glaubhaft, glaub- würdig	beneficiary	- Nutznießer, Begünstigte(r)
		benefit	- Nutzen, Gewinn
to believe	- glauben, meinen	to benefit from	- Nutzen ziehen aus
believer	- Gläubige(r) [Religion]	additional benefits	- Zusatzleistungen
*dis*belief	- Unglaube, Zweifel	*un*employment benefit	- Arbeitslosenunter- stützung
*un*believable	- unglaublich		

care	- Sorgfalt, Pflege	common(ly)	- gemeinsam
to care for	- sorgen für, mögen		- gewöhnlich
careful(ly)	- sorgfältig, vorsichtig		- häufig, normal
care*less*(ly)	- unvorsichtig, fahrlässig	to have something	
care*less*ness	- Fahrlässigkeit, Unvorsicht	in common	- etwas gemeinsam haben
		Common Market	- Gemeinsamer Markt
caring	- mitfühlend, engagiert, sozial	European Community	- Europäische Gemeinschaft
		the House of	
carriage	- Beförderung	Commons	- das britische Unterhaus
	- Fracht, Fuhrlohn	communal	- Gemeinde-
	- Wagen		- Gemeinschafts-
carriage return	- Zeilenschaltung	commune	- Gemeinde, Gebietskörperschaft
carrier	- Transportunternehmen, Frachtführer, Spediteur, Spedition	community	- Gemeinde, Gemeinschaft
to carry	- tragen, befördern	to communicate	- benachrichtigen, kommunizieren
amount carried forward	- Übertrag	communication	- Nachricht, Mitteilung,
carried forward	- auf einem Konto vorgetragen		- Verkehr, Verständigung - Kommunikation
carrying capacity	- Tragkraft	communicative	- mitteilsam
to carry out	- ausführen, durchführen	to compete	- konkurrieren
to carry over	- übertragen	to compete for	- sich mitbewerben um
		to compete with	- wetteifern mit
to cease	- aufhören, erlöschen	competent	- kompetent, fähig
to cease from doing	- ablassen von	competently	- geschickt, kompetent
ceaseless(ly)	- endlos, unaufhörlich	competition	- Mitbewerb, Konkurrenz
to cede	- abtreten, überlassen	competitive(ly)	- wettbewerbs-, konkurrenzfähig
cession (to)	- Abtretung (an)		
*in*cessantly	- unaufhörlich	competitiveness	- Wettbewerbs-, Konkurrenzfähigkeit
charge	- Belastung	competitive society	- Leistungsgesellschaft
	- Preis, Kosten, Unkosten	competitor	- Mitbewerber(in), Konkurrent(in)
charge account	- Kundenkreditkonto		
free of charge	- kostenlos	to complain	- klagen
to charge	- belasten, beladen	to complain of/about	- sich beschweren/beklagen über, reklamieren
	- berechnen		
to charge with	- beauftragen mit, zur Last legen	to complain of a headache	- über Kopfschmerzen klagen
to *dis*charge	- entlasten, entladen	to complain about the noise	- sich über den Lärm beschweren
	- entlassen		
choice [n]	- Wahl, Auswahl	complainant	- Kläger(in), Beschwerdeführer(in)
choice [adj]	- erstklassig, auserlesen		
to choose	- wählen	complaint	- Beschwerde, Reklamation, Mängelrüge
choosey	- wählerisch		

complete(ly)	- vollständig, vollkommen - vollzählig - beendet, fertig	considering *in*considerate(ly)	- wenn man bedenkt - rücksichtslos, unaufmerksam
to complete	- vervollständigen - beenden	to consign	- übergeben, übersenden, konsignieren
to complete a form	- ein Formular ausfüllen	consigned stock	- Kommissionslager
completeness	- Vollständigkeit, Vollkommenheit	consignable	- versendungsfähig
completion	- Vollendung, Fertigstellung - Vervollständigung - Erfüllung	consignation	- Übersendung von Ware, Konsignation, Konsignationsgeschäft
		consignee	- Empfänger(in)
*in*complete	- unvollständig	consignment	- Sendung, Warenlieferung - Verkauf auf Rechnung des Eigentümers
to concede	- anerkennen, bewilligen, zugestehen - aufgeben, abgeben	consignment/ consigned goods	- Konsignationswaren
to concede a point	- in einem Punkt nachgeben	consignment note	- Frachtbrief
concession	- Zugeständnis, Bewilligung	consignor	- Absender(in)
concessionaire	- Konzessionär	to consult	- um Rat fragen
concessionary	- Konzessions-	consultancy	- Beratungsbüro, Unternehmensberatung
to conclude	- beenden, abschließen - beschließen - folgern, schließen	consultant	- Berater(in)
		consultation	- Beratung, Rücksprache
		consultative management	- Betriebsführung mittels Komitees
to conclude a contract/deal	- einen Vertrag/ein Geschäft abschließen	consulting engineer	- technische(r) Berater(in)
conclusion	- Abschluß, Beschluß, Beschlußfassung - Folgerung	consulting hours	- Sprechstunde
		consumable	- verbrauchbar
conclusive(ly)	- beweiskräftig, maßgeblich, triftig	to consume	- verbrauchen
		consumer	- Verbraucher(in), Konsument(in)
to confide (in)	- anvertrauen	consumption	- Verbrauch
confidence	- Vertrauen, Zuversicht		
confident(ly)	- zuversichtlich	continual(ly)	- fortwährend, unaufhörlich
confidential(ly)	- vertraulich	continuance	- Fortdauer
to consider	- in Betracht ziehen, denken an	continuation	- Fortsetzung, Prolongation
considerable (-ably)	- beträchtlich	to continue	- fortfahren, prolongieren
considerate(ly)	- überlegt, wohldurchdacht	continued	- fortgesetzt
		continuing	- dauernd, ständig
considerate to/ towards	- aufmerksam, rücksichtsvoll (gegen)	continuity	- Stetigkeit, Kontinuität
		continuous(ly)	- stetig, fortlaufend
consideration	- Erwägung, Überlegung - Berücksichtigung, Rücksicht	continuum	- zusammenhängende Reihe von Elementen - Kontinuum

to *dis*continue	- aufhören, einstellen	courage	- Mut
		courageous(ly)	- mutig
to controvert	- bestreiten, widerlegen	to encourage	- ermutigen
controversial(ly)	- strittig	to *dis*courage	- entmutigen
controversy	- Streit, Auseinander-setzung	cover	- Decke, Deckel
			- Überzug, Bezug
			- Hülle, Schutzumschlag
to convene	- versammeln, einberufen	under the same cover	- mit gleicher Post
convenience	- Angemessenheit	under separate cover	- mit separater Post
	- Annehmlichkeit, Be-quemlichkeit	to cover	- bedecken
			- enthalten, einschließen, erfassen
at your earliest convenience	- umgehend, sobald wie möglich		
convenient(ly)	- passend, schicklich	to cover up	- verdecken
convention	- Abkommen, Tagung, Vertrag	covering letter	- Begleitbrief
		covering the cost	- Kosten decken
		cover note	- Deckungskarte
to correspond (with)	- übereinstimmen (mit)	to *un*cover	- aufdecken
	- an jemanden schreiben	aber: to *dis*cover	- entdecken
correspondence	- Übereinstimmung		
	- Korrespondenz, Brief-wechsel	critic	- Kritiker(in)
		critical(ly)	- kritisch
		criticism	- Kritik
correspondent	- Korrespondent(in), Kunde/Kundin	to criticize	- kritisieren
		critique	- kritische Besprechung oder Abhandlung
correspondent bank	- Bank, mit der man in Verbindung steht		
		*un*critical	- unkritisch
correspondent to a thing	- einer Sache ent-sprechend		
		custom	- Brauch, Gewohnheit, Sitte
correspondent with	- übereinstimmend mit		
corresponding(ly)	- entsprechend	customary	- gebräuchlich, alther-gebracht, handelsüblich
corrupt	- korrupt, verderbt, ver-dorben		
		customer	- Kunde, Kundin
to corrupt	- bestechen	to customize	- speziell anfertigen
corruptible	- bestechlich, verderblich	custom-made	- auf Bestellung/Wunsch des Kunden angefertigt
corruptibility	- Bestechlichkeit		
corruption	- Bestechung, Verderb-nis, Verführung, Ver-fälschung	customs ...	- Zoll- ...
		customs authorities	- Zollbehörde
		customs barrier	- Zollschranke
corruptive(ly)	- verderbend	customs clearance	- Zollabfertigung
corruptiveness	- Verderbtheit	customs declaration	- Zollerklärung
*in*corruptible	- unbestechlich	customs duty	- Zollabgabe

damage	- Beschädigung, Benachteiligung	definitely	- zweifellos
to damage	- schädigen, beschädigen	definiteness	- Bestimmtheit
damaged	- schadhaft, defekt	*in*definite	- unbestimmt, unbegrenzt
damages	- Entschädigungssumme	*in*definitely	- auf unbegrenzte Zeit
to claim damages	- Schadensersatz fordern	to deliver	- liefern, zustellen
deceit	- Täuschung, Betrug, List		- befreien
deceitful(ly)	- hinterlistig, betrügerisch, falsch	deliverance	- Befreiung
		deliverer	- Lieferant(in), Retter(in)
deceivable	- leicht zu betrügen, zu täuschen	delivery	- Lieferung, Zustellung
		delivery service	- Zustelldienst
to deceive	- täuschen, betrügen	to depend on	- abhängen von
to decide	- sich entscheiden, bestimmen	dependability	- Verläßlichkeit, Zuverlässigkeit
decided(ly)	- bestimmt, entschieden	dependable (-ably)	- verläßlich, zuverlässig
decider	- Entscheidungsspiel	dependant	- Unterhaltsberechtigte(r), Abhängige(r)
decision	- Entscheidung, Beschluß	dependence	- Abhängigkeit
decision-makers, decision-making people	- Leute, die Entscheidungen treffen	dependency	- Abhängigkeit, Zusammenhang
court decision	- Gerichtsentscheidung	dependencies	- Schutzgebiete, Kolonien
decisive(ly)	- entscheidend, ausschlaggebend, maßgeblich, maßgebend	dependent (on)	- abhängig (von), unselbständig
		*in*dependence	- Unabhängigkeit
decisiveness	- Entschiedenheit, Entschlossenheit	*in*dependent	- unabhängig
defect	- Fehler, Mangel	deposit	- Geldeinlage
to defect	- überlaufen, sich absetzen	to deposit	- deponieren
		depositary	- Treuhänder(in)
defection	- Überlaufen	depositor	- Depotkunde,-kundin, Hinterleger(in)
defective(ly)	- fehlerhaft		
defectiveness	- Fehlerhaftigkeit	depository	- Hinterlegungsstelle
defector	- Überläufer(in)	deposits	- Depositengelder
		depot	- Depot, Verwahrungsort
to define	- definieren, genau erklären	to describe	- beschreiben, bezeichnen
	- genau bezeichnen	description	- Beschreibung, Bezeichnung
definable	- definierbar, erklärbar		
definition	- genaue Erklärung, Begriffsbestimmung	descriptive	- beschreibend, darstellend
*in*definable	- undefinierbar	*in*describable	- unbeschreiblich, fürchterlich
*un*defined	- nicht definiert, unbestimmt		
definite, definitive	- bestimmt, fest, endgültig	determinable	- bestimmbar
			- (juristisch) befristet

determinant	- entscheidender Faktor	diminutive [adj]	- klein, winzig,
determinate	- bestimmt, begrenzt	diminutive [n]	- Verkleinerungsform
determination	- Bestimmung, Entschlossenheit	diminutiveness	- Winzigkeit
	- Festlegung, Festsetzung	direct(ly)	- unmittelbar, direkt
to determine	- bestimmen	direct from/to	- direkt von/nach
determined	- entschlossen	to direct	- anordnen, anweisen, steuern
determinedly	- voller Entschlossenheit		
co-determination	- Mitbestimmung	to direct a letter to	- einen Brief richten an, adressieren
self-determination	- Selbstbestimmung		
*in*determinable	- unbestimmbar	direction	- Anordnung, Anweisung
*in*determinate(ly)	- unbestimmt, vage		- Lenkung, Richtung
*in*determination	- Unentschlossenheit	directive	- Anordnung, Anweisung, Richtlinie
to develop	- entwickeln	directness	- Direktheit, Offenheit
developer	- Gründstückserschließer(in)	director	- Direktor(in), Aufsichtsratsmitglied
	- Entwickler [Foto]	directorate	- Direktorium, Vorstand, Dienstzeit
developing countries	- Entwicklungsländer		
development	- Entwicklung	directory	- Adreßbuch
development aid	- Entwicklungshilfe	telephone directory	- Telefonbuch
		*in*direct(ly)	- indirekt
to devise	- ausdenken, ersinnen		
	- hinterlassen, vererben (von Grundstücken bzw. unbeweglichen Sachen)	distributable	- ausschüttungsfähig, verteilungsfähig
		to distribute	- verteilen, verbreiten, vertreiben
devisee	- Vermächtnisempfänger(in) (von unbeweglichen Sachen)	distributed profit	- ausgeschütteter Gewinn
		distribution	- Ausschüttung, Verteilung, Vertrieb
devisor	- Erblasser(in) (von unbeweglichen Sachen)	distribution agency	- Vertriebsagentur
		distributor	- Händler(in), Wiederverkäufer(in), Verteiler(in)
Merke: device	- Gerät		
		diverse	- mehrere, etliche
to differ (from)	- sich unterscheiden (von)		- verschiedenartig, mannigfaltig
difference	- Unterschied		
different	- verschieden, anders	diversification	- Diversifikation des Verkaufsprogramms
differential	- differential, Unterscheidungs-		
		to diversify	- diversifizieren
differential gear	- Differentialgetriebe	diversion	- Ablenkung, Zeitvertreib
to differentiate	- unterscheiden, differenzieren		- Umleitung (Verkehr)
		diversity	- Verschiedenheit, Mannigfaltigkeit
differentiation	- Differenzierung, Unterscheidung		
		to divert	- ablenken, umleiten
to diminish	- abnehmen, verkleinern	to divide	- abtrennen, teilen
diminution	- Abnahme, Schmälerung, Verkleinerung, Verminderung	dividend	- Gewinnanteil, Dividende
			- Dividend

divisible	- teilbar, zerlegbar	to draft	- abfassen, entwerfen
divisibility	- Teilbarkeit, Trennbarkeit	to draw	- zeichnen
division	- Teilung, Abteilung		- ausstellen von Urkunden, (insbesondere von Wechseln und Schecks) trassieren
division of labour	- Arbeitsteilung		
divisor	- Divisor, Teiler		
*in*divisible	- unteilbar		- ziehen
		drawee	- Bezogener, Akzeptant von Schecks und Wechseln
doubt	- Zweifel, Bedenken, Ungewißheit		
to doubt	- anzweifeln, zweifeln	drawer	- Aussteller von Schecks und Wechseln
doubter	- Zweifler		
doubtful(ly)	- bedenklich, zweifelhaft, zweifelnd		- Schublade, Schubfach
		drawing	- Zeichnung, Konstruktionszeichnung
doubtfulness	- Zweifelhaftigkeit, Bedenklichkeit		
		drawings	- Zeichnungen
doubt*less*(ly)	- zweifelsohne, fraglos		- Entnahmen
*un*doubted(ly)	- zweifellos, unbestritten		
		durable (-ably)	- dauerhaft
draft	- Entwurf	durables	- Gebrauchsgüter
	- Tratte, gezogener Wechsel	durability	- Dauerhaftigkeit
		duration	- Dauer, Laufzeit

e

economic	- volkswirtschaftlich, nationalökonomisch	to edit	- herausgeben (von Büchern)
	- wirtschaftlich, Wirtschafts-		- (Text) redigieren, druckfertig machen
economical(ly)	- haushälterisch, sparsam, ökonomisch	edition	- Auflage (eines Buches), Ausgabe
economically [adv]	- in volkswirtschaftlicher Hinsicht	editor	- Herausgeber(in)
			- Redakteur(in)
economics	- (Volks)Wirtschaftslehre	editorial	- Leitartikel
economist	- Volkswirtschaftler(in), Wirtschaftspolitiker(in)	editor-in-chief	- Chefredakteur(in)
to economize	- rationalisieren	effect	- Auswirkung, Geltung, Wirkung
economizing	- Rationalisierung		
economy	- Wirtschaft (als Gesamtheit)	in effect	- in Wirklichkeit
		to the effect	- dem Sinne nach, des Inhalts
	- Sparsamkeit, Kosteneinsparung	to effect	- ausführen, bewirken, wirken
economy class	- Touristenklasse		
economy size	- Sparpackung	effective(ly)	- wirksam, gültig, nachhaltig
eastern/western economies	- östliche/westliche Wirtschaftssysteme		
		effectiveness	- Wirksamkeit
economies	- Ersparnisse, Einsparungen	effects (personal effects)	- Habe, Effekten, bewegliches Eigentum

effectual(ly)	- wirksam	to enter	- eintreten, herein-kommen, betreten
to effectuate	- bewirken		- buchen, eintragen
*in*effective	- unwirksam	to enter into negotiations	- in Verhandlungen eintreten
efficacious(ly)	- wirksam, kräftig	entrance (into)	- Eingang, Einfahrt, Einlaß, Zutritt
efficacy	- Wirksamkeit		
efficiency	- Leistungsfähigkeit, Tüchtigkeit	entrance to an office	- Antritt eines Amtes
efficient(ly)	- leistungsfähig	entrance fee	- Eintrittsgebühr
*in*efficiency	- Unzulänglichkeit	entry	- Eintritt
*in*efficient	- unzulänglich		- Eingang von Geldern
Merke: deficiency	- Mangel(haftigkeit), Defizit, Fehlbetrag, Schwäche		- Buchung
		entry into	- Beitritt
		entry form	- Anmeldeformular
to embark (for)	- einschiffen, verladen (nach)	to err	- irren
to embark on	- anfangen, sich einlassen (in/auf)	erratic(ally)	- unberechenbar, ziellos, unregelmäßig
embarkation	- Einschiffung	erratum	- Druckfehler
to *dis*embark	- ausschiffen	erroneous(ly)	- irrig, irrtümlich, irrtümlicherweise, falsch
emphasis	- Nachdruck		
to emphasize	- betonen (mit Nachdruck)	error	- Irrtum, Fehler
emphatic(ally)	- nachdrücklich, betont, deutlich, eindringlich	estimate	- Berechnung, Kostenvoranschlag, Schätzung
to employ	- einstellen, beschäftigen	to estimate	- schätzen
	- anwenden, benutzen	estimated	- überschlägig, geschätzt
employee	- Angestellte(r), Arbeitnehmer(in)	estimation	- (Ein)Schätzung, Achtung, Veranschlagung
employees	- Belegschaft, Mitarbeiter		- Meinung, Ansicht
employed	- berufstätig	to hold in estimation	- hochschätzen
employer	- Arbeitgeber(in)	in my estimation	- meiner Meinung /Ansicht nach
employers' association	- Arbeitgeberverband		
*un*employed	- arbeitslos		
*un*employment benefit	- Arbeitslosenunterstützung	to evade	- ausweichen, umgehen
		evasion	- Ausflucht
endorsable	- indossierbar	tax evasion	- Steuerumgehung
to endorse (on)	- auf der Rückseite beschreiben, vermerken	evasive(ly)	- ausweichend
	- girieren, indossieren	to exceed	- überschreiten, übertreffen, übersteigen
endorsee	- Girat, Indossat, Giratar, Indossatar	excess	- Übermaß, Überschreitung, Überschuß
endorsement	- Indossament, Weitergabevermerk, Giro	to be in excess	- hinausgehen über
full endorsement	- Vollindossament	excess baggage/ luggage	- Übergewicht (im Flugverkehr)
endorser	- Indossant, Girant	excessive(ly)	- übermäßig, übertrieben
Merke: alle diese Wörter können am Anfang auch mit "i" geschrieben werden.		excessiveness	- Übermäßigkeit

to exclude	- ausschließen	expenditures	- Auslagen, Kosten
excluding	- ausschließlich	expense	- Ausgabe, Aufwand
exclusion	- Ausschluß	at your expense	- auf Ihre Kosten
exclusive	- erstklassig, exklusiv	expensed	- über Aufwand abgebucht
exclusive(ly)	- ausschließlich		
exclusive of/ excluding VAT	- ausschließlich Mehrwertsteuer	expenses	- Spesen, Unkosten, Auslagen
exclusively entitled	- alleinberechtigt	expensive(ly)	- aufwendig, teuer, kostspielig
exclusivity stipulation	- Ausschlußklausel, Sperrklausel		
		*in*expensive	- nicht teuer, billig
to execute	- ausführen, erledigen	to explain	- erklären
	- vollziehen, hinrichten	explainable	- erklärbar
execution	- Ausführung, Verrichtung	explanation	- Erklärung, Erläuterung
		explanatory (-orily)	- erläuternd
	- Vollzug, Hinrichtung	explicable	- erklärlich
compulsory execution	- Zwangsvollstreckung		
executive	- Führungskraft, leitende(r) Angestellte(r)	exposal	- Aussetzung
		to expose	- aufdecken
executor, executrix	- (Testaments)Vollstrecker(in)		- belichten
		to expose to	- (einer Sache) aussetzen
executory	- Vollziehungs-, Ausübungs-	exposition	- Darlegung
			- Ausstellung
		expositive, expository	- klärend, erläuternd
to exhibit	- ausstellen (von Waren)	expositor	- Ausleger, Erklärer, Erläuterer
exhibit	- Ausstellungsgegenstand		
	- Beweismittel	exposure	- Belichtung(szeit)
exhibition	- Ausstellung, Messe		- Aufnahme
exhibitor	- Aussteller(in)		- (medizinisch) Frei-, Bloßlegung
to expand	- ausbreiten, ausdehnen		- Aussetzung (z. B. von Kind)
expander	- Expander		
expanse	- weiter Raum, Ausdehnung		- (bildlich) Bloßstellung, Enthüllung, Entlarvung
expansible	- ausdehnbar		
expansion	- Ausbreitung, Ausdehnung, Expansion	death by exposure	- Tod durch Erfrieren
		to extend	- ausdehnen, verlängern
expansionary	- expansiv		- ausstrecken
expansive(ly)	- Ausdehnungs-, ausgedehnt, ausdehnungsfähig		- sich erstrecken
		extension	- Ausdehnung, Verlängerung
	- mitteilsam, gesprächig		- [Telefon] Nebenanschluß, Apparat
expansiveness	- Ausdehnungsfähigkeit		
		extension lead	- Verlängerungsschnur
to expend	- ausgeben (Geld), aufwenden	extensive(ly)	- ausgedehnt
		extensiveness	- Ausdehnung, Weite
expenditure	- Ausgabe, Aufwand	extent	- Ausmaß

f

facile	- einfach	false(ly)	- falsch
	- oberflächlich, banal	falseness	- Falschheit
to facilitate	- erleichtern		- Unwahrheit, Lüge
facilitation	- Erleichterung, Förderung	falsifiable	- Verrat, Betrug - widerlegbar
facilities	- Erleichterungen	falsification	- Fälschung, Verfälschung
	- Anlagen, Einrichtungen	falsifier to falsify	- Fälscher(in) - fälschen, verfälschen
production facilities	- Produktionsanlagen	falsity	- Unrichtigkeit, Falschheit
facility	- Leichtigkeit		- Unaufrichtigkeit
	- günstige Gelegenheit, Möglichkeit	fault faultiness	- Fehler, Mangel - Fehlerhaftigkeit, Mangelhaftigkeit
to fail	- etwas nicht tun, versäumen	faulty	- fehlerhaft, mangelhaft
	- versagen, scheitern	fault*less*(ly)	- fehlerfrei, tadellos
	- [bei Prüfung] durchfallen	fund	- Fond, Geldquelle - Deckung
	- [Geräte] ausfallen, nicht arbeiten	to fund	- anlegen, investieren - bezahlen, finanzieren
failing	- Schwäche, Fehler	funds	- Gelder, Kapital, Mittel
fail-safe	- (ab)gesichert	Consolidated Fund	- konsolidierter Staats-
failure	- Fehlschlag, Mißerfolg		fond, ordentlicher
	- Versager(in)		Staatshaushalt [GB]
	- Ausfall (eines Geräts)	funded	- fundiert, verbrieft
	- Verschlechterung		

g

grade	- Güteklasse, Klassenstufe	gradual(ly)	- allmählich, nach und nach
to grade	- (nach Größe, Rang usw.) einteilen, sortieren	graduate to graduate	- Akademiker(in) - einteilen, abstufen - graduieren
	- abstufen, einteilen	graduated	- mit Maßeinteilung
	- (nach Gehalt) einstufen		- graduiert
graded	- gestaffelt	graduated income tax	- abgestufte Einkommensteuer
graded tax	- Stufensteuer		
gradient	- Neigung, Steigung, Gefälle	graduation	- Maßeinteilung - (Universitäts)Abschluß
grading	- Klassifizierung, Klassifikation	*de*gradation to *de*grade	- Erniedrigung - erniedrigen

67

identical(ly)	- identisch	informant	- Informant(in), Gewährsperson
identification	- Identifizierung, Legitimation	information [kein Plural]	- Auskunft, Information, Nachricht
to identify	- identifizieren, legitimieren	informative	- informativ, aufschlußreich
to identify oneself	- sich ausweisen	informed	- informiert, unterrichtet, gebildet
identity	- Identität	informer	- Informant(in), Denunziant(in)
ignorance	- Unwissenheit		
ignorant	- unwissend, ungebildet	*un*informed	- nicht/schlecht unterrichtet
to be ignorant of	- etwas nicht kennen, nicht wissen		
ignorantly	- unwissentlich, fälschlicherweise	*un*informative	- nicht/wenig informativ
		Merke: informal	- inoffiziell
to ignore	- ignorieren, nicht beachten	insurable	- versicherbar
		insurance	- Versicherung
imitable	- nachahmbar, imitierbar	insurance policy	- Versicherungspolice
to imitate	- nachmachen, nachahmen	to insure	- versichern
	- fälschen (Unterschrift)	to insure oneself against	- sich versichern gegen
imitation	- Nachahmung, Imitation	insurer	- Versicherungsgeber(in), Versicherer
imitation jewellery	- unechter Schmuck		
imitative	- nachahmend, imitierend	to introduce a person	- eine Person vorstellen
		to introduce an article	- einen Artikel einführen
imitator	- Nachahmer, Imitator	introduction	- Vorstellung, Einführung
		introductory offer	- Einführungsangebot
to impress	- beeindrucken, eindrücken	to invent	- erfinden
to be impressed by	- beeindruckt sein	invention	- Erfindung
impression	- Eindruck, auch bildlich	inventive	- erfinderisch, einfallsreich
		inventor	- Erfinder(in)
to be under the impression	- den Eindruck haben	inventory	- Bestandsverzeichnis, Lagerbestände
to make an impression	- Eindruck machen		
impressionable	- für Eindrücke empfänglich	to invest	- anlegen, investieren
		investment	- Anlage von Kapital
impressive(ly)	- eindrucksvoll, imponierend	investor	- Geldanleger(in), Investor(in)
impressiveness	- das Eindrucksvolle		
*un*impressed	- unbeeindruckt	to investigate	- ermitteln, nachforschen
*un*impressive	- unbeeindruckend	investigation	- Ermittlung, Nachforschung
to inform	- benachrichten, informieren	investigator	- Rechercheur(in), Untersuchende(r)

j

to join	- zusammenfügen, verbinden, vereinigen - beitreten, anschließen, eintreten	judiciousness	- Einsicht, Klugheit
		juridical(ly)	- juristisch
		jurisdiction	- Gerichtsbarkeit - Gerichtsbezirk, Zuständigkeitsbereich
joining	- Beitritt, Eintritt		
joint [n]	- Verbindung(sstück)		
joint [adj]	- gemeinschaftlich, gemeinsam	jurisprudence	- Rechtswissenschaft
		juror	- Geschworene(r), Schöffe, Schöffin - Preisrichter(in)
joint-stock	- Aktienkapital		
Joint Stock Companies Act	- Aktiengesetz	jury, jurymen	- Geschworene
joint venture	- gemeinsames Handelsunternehmen, Joint Venture	just	- gerecht
		justifiable (-ably)	- begründbar, vertretbar
		justifiability	- Vertretbarkeit, Entschuldbarkeit
jointly and severally	- gesamtschuldnerisch, gemeinschaftlich, solidarisch	justification	- Begründung
		justice	- Gerechtigkeit - Richter(in) (eines übergeordneten Gerichts)
judge	- Richter(in)		
to judge	- richten		
to judge from	- urteilen nach	to justify	- rechtfertigen, begründen - justieren, im Blocksatz setzen
to be judged by	- beurteilt werden nach		
judgement	- Urteil, Ermessen,		
to *mis*judge	- falsch einschätzen	justly	- mit Recht - verdientermaßen
*mis*judgement	- Fehleinschätzung		
		*un*just	- ungerecht
judicature	- Gerichtswesen	*un*justifiable	- nicht zu rechtfertigen, unverantwortlich
judicial(ly)	- richterlich		
judiciary	- Gerichtswesen, Richterstand	*un*justified	- ungerechtfertigt, unberechtigt
judicious(ly)	- klug, einsichtsvoll, vernünftig	*in*justice, *un*justness	- Ungerechtigkeit

k

to know	- wissen - kennen	knowingly	- wissentlich, absichtlich
		knowledge [kein Plural]	- Kenntnisse
to know about	- sich auskennen	knowledgable	- kenntnisreich, viel wissend
knowable	- was man wissen kann		
know-how	- Praxis, Know-how	known	- bekannt, anerkannt
knowing(ly)	- wissend, verständnisvoll	well-known	- sehr bekannt, wohlbekannt

law	- Gesetz	legitimacy	- Rechtmäßigkeit, Ehelichkeit
lawful(ly)	- gesetzmäßig, rechtlich	legitimate	- ehelich, rechtmäßig
lawfulness	- Gesetzmäßigkeit, Rechtlichkeit	*il*legitimacy	- Unehelichkeit, Ungesetzlichkeit
law*less*(ly)	- rechtswidrig	*il*legitimate	- unehelich, unrechtmäßig
law*less*ness	- Ungesetzlichkeit		
lawmaker	- Gesetzgeber		
lawsuit	- Prozeß, Rechtsstreit	liquid	- flüssig
lawyer	- Advokat(in), Rechtsanwalt,-wältin, Justiziar(in)		- verfügbar
		to liquidate	- ablösen (Schuld), auflösen, liquidieren
legal(ly)	- gesetzlich, rechtlich, legal	liquidation	- Ablösung, Löschung von Schuld, Tilgung, Liquidierung
legality	- Gesetzmäßigkeit, Rechtmäßigkeit		
legalization	- Beglaubigung, Beurkundung, Legalisierung	liquidator	- Liquidator, Abwickler
		liquidity	- Liquidität
to legalize	- beglaubigen, legalisieren	litigant	- Prozeßpartei
		to litigate	- prozessieren
*il*legal(ly)	- ungesetzlich, rechtswidrig, illegal, widerrechtlich	litigation	- Prozeß, Streitsache
		litigious(ly)	- prozeßsüchtig, strittig
		to lose	- verlieren
*il*legality	- Ungesetzmäßigkeit, Rechtswidrigkeit	loser	- Verlierer(in)
		loss	- Verlust
		a loss sustained, a loss incurred	- ein erlittener Schaden, Verlust
to legislate	- ein Gesetz verabschieden		
legislation	- Gesetzgebung	any loss incurred	- eventuelle Schäden, Verluste
legislative	- gesetzgebend		
legislator	- Gesetzgeber	Lost Property Office	- Fundbüro

m

to maintain	- aufrechterhalten - instandsetzen, warten	memo (memorandum)	- Aktennotiz
maintenance	- Aufrechterhaltung, Erhaltung - Instandhaltung, Wartung	memoirs	- Denkschrift, Lebenserinnerungen, Memoiren
		memorable	- unvergeßlich, erinnerungswürdig
maintenance program(me)	- Pflegeplan, Wartungsplan	memorably	- bemerkenswert
		memorial	- Denkmal, Ehrenmal, Andenken
to manage	- verwalten, regeln - zurechtkommen, es schaffen	to memorize	- auswendig lernen, sich merken
		memory	- Gedächtnis, Erinnerung - Speicher, Informationsspeicher
manageable	- leicht zu handhaben		
management	- Leitung, Führung, Management	from memory	- auswendig
		to commemorate	- jemandes gedenken
manager	- (Abteilungs)Leiter(in)	commemoration	- Gedächtnisfeier
general manager	- Geschäftsführer(in)		
manageress	- Leiterin, Abteilungsleiterin	mercantile	- kaufmännisch, merkantil
managerial	- leitend	merchandise	- Handelsware
managing director	- leitende(r) Direktor(in)	merchandising	- Ausübung der Absatzfunktionen
*mis*management	- schlechte Geschäftsführung, Mißmanagement	merchant	- Kaufmann, -frau, Händler(in)

n

negotiable	- verkäuflich - übertragbar, begebbar	note	- Notiz, Anmerkung
		to note	- bemerken, zur Kenntnis nehmen, beachten
negotiability	- Übertragbarkeit		
to negotiate	- verhandeln - übertragen, negoziieren - bewältigen (Hindernis)	to note down	- aufschreiben, notieren
		notice	- Benachrichtung, Mitteilung - Bekanntmachung - Kündigung
negotiation	- Verhandlung - Übertragung, Negoziierung	to give notice	- kündigen
		noticeable	- erkennbar
negotiator	- Unterhändler(in)	noticeably	- deutlich
non-negotiable	- nicht übertragbar, nicht begebbar	notifiable	- meldepflichtig
		notification	- Benachrichtigung, Meldung
a non-negotiable bill of lading	- ein nicht begebbares Konossement	to notify	- benachrichtigen

obedience	- Gehorsam	office	- Amt, Büro
obedient(ly)	- gehorsam	officer	- Angestellte(r) im öffentlichen Dienst, Beamter, Beamtin,
in obedience to your wishes	- gemäß/entsprechend Ihren Wünschen		- Offizier
to obey	- befolgen, gehorchen		
*dis*obedience	- Nichtbefolgung	official	- Beamter, Beamtin
*dis*obedient (to)	- ungehorsam (gegen)	official(ly)	- amtlich, dienstlich, offiziell
*dis*obey	- einen Befehl nicht beachten	officialdom	- Bürokratismus, Beamtentum
occupancy	- Besitzergreifung, Aneignung	officialese	- Amtsdeutsch, Beamtendeutsch
occupant	- Besitzer(in), Inhaber(in)	officialism	- Bürokratismus
		to officiate	- amtieren
	- Bewohner(in)	officious(ly)	- übertrieben diensteifrig
occupation	- Beruf	*un*official	- inoffiziell
occupational(ly)	- beruflich		
occupier	- Bewohner(in), Inhaber(in)	omissible	- auszulassend, auslaßbar, kann weggelassen werden
to occupy	- aneignen, besetzen, innehaben	omission	- Auslassung, Versäumnis, Unterlassung
to occupy oneself with	- sich beschäftigen mit	to omit	- auslassen, versäumen, unterlassen
to be occupied with	- sich befassen mit		
offence	- Beleidigung, Verletzung	to operate	- betreiben, handhaben
to offend (against)	- verstoßen (gegen), beleidigen, verletzen	to operate on	- einwirken auf
			- operieren
offender	- Straffällige(r), Täter(in)	operation	- Arbeitsgang
offensive(ly)	- offensiv, Angriffs-		- Tätigkeit
	- beleidigend, anstoßerregend		- Operation
		operational(ly)	- betriebsbereit, Betriebs-
offensiveness	- das Beleidigende, Anstößige	operator	- Bediener(in) einer Maschine, Telefonvermittlung
	- Widerlichkeit, Ekelhaftigkeit		

p

permissible (-ibly)	- erlaubt, zulässig	to precede	- vorausgehen
permissibility	- Zulässigkeit	precedence	- Vorrang, Priorität
permission	- Bewilligung, Genehmigung	to take precedence over	- Vorrang haben vor
permissive	- nachgiebig	precedent	- Präzedenzfall
permissiveness	- Nachgiebigkeit	preceding	- vorhergehend
permit	- Bewilligung, Genehmigung		
to permit	- erlauben, bewilligen	to prefer (to)	- vorziehen, begünstigen
		preference	- Bevorzugung, Präferenz, Vergünstigung
person	- Person, Einzelwesen	preferential	- vorzugsweise, bevorrechtigt
personable	- sympathisch		
personal (data)	- persönlich(e Daten)	preferential tariffs	- Vorzugszölle
personality	- Persönlichkeit	preferred	- bevorzugt
to personalize	- personifizieren, typisieren	nonpreferential	- ohne Vorzug
personally	- persönlich, selbst		
personalty	- Mobiliarvermögen	prejudice	- Vorurteil, Befangenheit
personification	- Verkörperung	prejudiced	- befangen, voreingenommen
to personify	- personifizieren, versinnbildlichen		
		prejudicial(ly)	- nachteilig, schädlich
personnel	- Belegschaft, Personal		
impersonal	- unpersönlich	to prescribe	- vorschreiben
			- verordnen, verfügen
plan	- Plan	prescribed	- vorgeschrieben, bestimmt
to plan	- planen		
planned economy	- Planwirtschaft	prescriptable	- verjährbar
planning	- Planung	prescription	- Vorschrift, Verordnung
			- Rezept, vorgeschriebene Medizin
polite(ly)	- höflich		
	- fein, verfeinert		- Verjährung
politeness	- Höflichkeit	prescriptive(ly)	- vorschreibend
impolite	- unhöflich	prescriptive right	- Gewohnheitsrecht
		prescriptive debt	- Verjährungsschuld
possibility	- Möglichkeit		
possibilities	- (Entwicklungs)Möglichkeiten	presumable (-ably)	- vermutlich, voraussichtlich
possible	- möglich	to presume	- annehmen, vermuten, voraussetzen
	- denkbar		
possibly	- möglicherweise	presumedly	- mutmaßlich
impossible	- unmöglich	presumption	- (meist)Anmaßung
		presumption (assumption)	- Annahme, Mutmaßung
postponable	- aufschiebbar		
postponability	- Verschiebbarkeit	presumptuous(ly)	- anmaßend, eingebildet
to postpone	- aufschieben, vertagen, verschieben		
postponed	- gestundet, verschoben		
postponement	- Aufschiebung, Verschiebung		

Merke:
Dr. Livingstone, I presume? I assume that the matter has been dealt with. – Dr. Livingstone, vermutlich? Ich nehme an, daß die Angelegenheit jetzt geregelt worden ist.

to prevail	- vorherrschen, ausschlaggebend sein	profiteering	- Preistreiberei, Wuchergeschäfte
prevalence	- allgemeine Gültigkeit, Vorherrschen	profits	- Ertrag, Nutzungen, Gewinn
prevalent	- allgemein gültig, vorherrschend	profit-sharing plan	- Gewinnbeteiligungsplan
		*un*profitable	- unrentabel, keinen Gewinn bringend
to prevent (from)	- verhindern, vermeiden, bewahren vor	promise	- Versprechen, Zusage
prevention	- Vorbeugung, Verhinderung	to promise	- versprechen, zusagen
preventive(ly)	- vorbeugend, präventiv	promisee	- Versprechungsempfänger(in)
		promising	- vielversprechend
procedure	- Verfahren, Vorgang	promisor	- Versprechungsgeber(in)
procedural review	- Organisationsprüfung	promissory	- verpflichtend
to proceed	- vorgehen, fortfahren, verfahren	promissory note	- Eigenwechsel, Promesse, Solawechsel, Schuldschein
proceeding	- Prozeß, gerichtliches Verfahren		
proceedings	- Akten, Sitzungsberichte	proper(ly)	- geeignet, richtig
proceeds	- Ertrag		- anständig, schicklich
			- eigen
process	- Verfahren	proper fraction	- echter Bruch
to process	- aufbereiten, bearbeiten	in the proper meaning	- genau genommen
processed	- bearbeitet	proper name	- Eigenname
processing	- Arbeitsablauf, Bearbeitung	*im*proper	- ungeeignet
text/word processing	- Textverarbeitung	proprietary	- jemandem gehörig, patentlich/gesetzlich geschützt
produce	- (landwirtschaftliche) Erzeugnisse		
to produce	- erzeugen	proprietor	- Eigentümer(in), Inhaber(in)
producer	- Hersteller(in), Produzent(in)	proprietorship	- Eigentum, Einzelunternehmung
product	- Erzeugnis	proprietory possession	- [US] Eigenbesitz
production	- Erzeugung, Herstellung	property	- Besitz
productive(ly)	- ertragreich, produktiv, - leistungsfähig	to prosper	- gedeihen, begünstigen, blühen [fig]
productivity	- Ertragsfähigkeit, Ergiebigkeit, Produktivität	prosperous(ly)	- glücklich, gedeihlich, günstig
*un*productive	- unproduktiv, unergiebig	prosperity	- Wohlstand
			- [US] blühendes Geschäft, Prosperität
profit	- Gewinn, Nutzen		
to profit	- Nutzen ziehen, verdienen	proof	- Beweis, Probeabzug
profitable	- einträglich, gewinnbringend	noise-proofing devices	- Lärmschutzeinrichtungen
profitability	- Wirtschaftlichkeit, Rentabilität	rust-proofing compound	- Rostschutzmittel
profiteer	- Geschäftemacher(in)		

to prove	- beweisen, sich erweisen	publicity	- Öffentlichkeit - Werbung
to provide (with)	- beschaffen, versehen (mit)	to publicize	- bekanntmachen, öffentlich bekanntgeben
provider	- Ernährer(in)	public relations	- Öffentlichkeitsarbeit - Public Relations
provision	- Vorkehrung - Rückstellung	to publish	- bekanntgeben - herausgeben, verlegen, veröffentlichen
provision clause	- Vorbehaltsklausel		
provisional(ly)	- vorläufig, behelfsmäßig	publisher	- Verleger(in), Herausgeber(in)
provisions	- Vorräte an Lebensmitteln	publishing house	- Verlag
		purpose	- Absicht, Zweck - Entschlossenheit
public(ly)	- öffentlich, gemeinnützig	on purpose	- absichtlich, mit Absicht
public	- Öffentlichkeit, Publikum	purpose-built	- spezialangefertigt
		purposeful(ly)	- entschlossen
publication	- Bekanntgabe, Bekanntmachung - Veröffentlichung	purposefulness	- Entschlossenheit
		purpose*less*	- sinnlos
		purposely	- absichtlich

r

real(ly)	- echt, wirklich	receipted bill	- quittierte Rechnung
real estate	- Grundstück, Immobilie	receipts	- Einkünfte, Einnahmen
reality	- Wirklichkeit	receivable	- offen
realizable, realisable	- realisierbar	receivables	- Außenstände
realization, realisation	- Erkenntnis, Verwirklichung	to receive	- erhalten - in Empfang nehmen
to realize	- einsehen, erkennen, - verwirklichen	receiver	- Empfänger(in) - (Telefon)Hörer - Übernehmer(in), Vergleichs-/Konkursverwalter(in)
realtor [US]	- Grundstücksmakler(in)		
realty	- unbewegliches Eigentum		
reason	- Grund, Begründung	receivership	- Konkursverwaltung
to reason	- vernünftig denken - urteilen	to go into receivership	- Konkurs machen
		reception	- Empfang, Rezeption
reasonable (-ably)	- angemessen, vernünftig	receptionist	- Empfangsdame, Empfangschef
reasonableness	- Angemessenheit, Vernünftigkeit	receptive(ly)	- aufnahmefähig
reasoning	- Beweisführung, Argumentation - Schließen, Urteilen	receptiveness, receptivity	- Aufnahmebereitschaft, Empfänglichkeit
		recipient	- Empfänger(in), Überweisungsempfänger(in)
receipt	- Erhalt - Quittung, Empfangsbestätigung	record [n]	- Akte, Aufzeichnung - Schallplatte

record [adj]	- Spitzen-	*de*regulation of prices	- Aufhebung der Preiskontrolle
to record	- aufzeichnen		
	- zu Protokoll nehmen, protokollieren	*ir*regular	- unregelmäßig
		*ir*regularity	- Unregelmäßigkeit
recordable	- eintragungsfähig		
recorder	- Diktiergerät, Aufnahmegerät	to relate	- erzählen, berichten
		to relate to	- sich beziehen auf
recording	- Aufzeichnung, Aufnahme	related	- verwandt
		relating to	- sich beziehend auf
records	- Archiv, Unterlagen	relation	- Verhältnis
		relations	- Beziehungen
to redeem	- ablösen (von Schuld)		- Verwandte
	- einlösen	relationship	- Beziehung
redeemable (-ably)	- ablösbar, tilgbar	relative [n]	- Verwandte(r)
redeemability	- Einlösbarkeit, Tilgbarkeit	relative [adj]	- relativ, bezüglich
		relative to	- sich beziehen auf
redemption	- Ablösung, Einlösung	relatively	- verhältnismäßig
register	- Register, Verzeichnis	relief	- Erleichterung
to register	- einschreiben		- Hilfe, Entlastung
	- in Register bringen		- Entschädigung
	- registrieren, bemerken		- Relief
registered	- eingeschrieben	in relief	- erhaben
by registered mail	- per Einschreiben	relief valve	- Ausgleichsventil
registrar	- Standesbeamte/-beamtin, Verwaltungsbeamte/-beamtin	to relieve	- abhelfen, entlasten,
			- befreien
			- unterstützen
registration	- Eintragung, Erfassung		
	- Anmeldung, Einschreibung	to remain	- übrigbleiben, verbleiben
		remainder	- Rest
registry	- Standesamt		- Restmenge
			- Anwartschaft (auf Grundbesitz)
regular(ly)	- gleichmäßig, ordentlich, regelmäßig		
		remainders	- Restbestände
regularity	- Ordnungsmäßigkeit, Regelmäßigkeit	remaining margin	- Restspanne
		remains	- Überbleibsel, Reste, Überreste
to regulate	- ordnen, regeln, einrichten, regulieren		
		to remit	- (Geld) überweisen
regulation	- Regulierung, Regelung, Vorschrift, Dienstvorschrift		- nachlassen (von Schulden)
			- remittieren
regulations	- Satzungen, Statuten, Dienstvorschriften	remittance	- Geldsendung, Überweisung von Geld
regulative(ly)	- regelnd		
regulator	- Regler, Regelvorrichtung	remittance advice	- Überweisungsanzeige
		remittance slip	- Überweisungsschein
regulatory statutes	- Ausführungsbestimmungen	remittee	- Überweisungsempfänger(in)
to *de*regulate	- von einschränkenden Bestimmungen befreien	remitter, remittor	- Geldübersender(in), Überweiser(in)

to repeat	- wiederholen	revocable	- widerrufbar
repeated(ly)	- wiederholt	revocation	- Aufhebung, Widerrufung
repeat order	- Nachbestellung, Wiederholungsauftrag	to revoke	- widerrufen, zurücknehmen
repetition	- Wiederholung	*ir*revocable	- unwiderruflich
repetitive	- sich wiederholend, wiederkehrend	rule	- Grundsatz, Norm - Regel, Vorschrift, Bestimmung
to reside	- wohnen	to rule	- herrschen
residence	- Aufenthalt - Wohnort, Residenz	ruled	- liniert
resident [n]	- Bewohner(in), Einwohner(in)	ruler	- Lineal - Herrscher(in)
resident [adj]	- ansässig	rules	- Spielregeln
residential area	- Wohngebiet	ruling [n]	- Gerichtsentscheidung
residential district	- Wohnsiedlung	ruling [adj]	- leitend, vorherrschend

S

safe	- Geldschrank, Safe	satisfactory (-orily)	- zufriedenstellend
safe(ly)	- sicher, geschützt	to satisfy	- zufriedenstellen
safeguard	- Schutz, Sicherheitsklausel	satisfying(ly)	- zufriedenstellend, befriedigend
to safeguard	- garantieren		- genügend, ausreichend
safeguarding	- Sicherstellung	*dis*satisfaction	- Unzufriedenheit
safekeeping	- Aufbewahrung	*dis*satisfied	- unzufrieden
safety	- Sicherheit	*un*satisfactory	- unbefriedigend, unerfreulich
for reasons of safety	- aus Sicherheitsgründen	*un*satisfying	- unbefriedigend
sale	- Absatz, Verkauf, Ausverkauf	savable	- zu retten, rettbar
for sale	- zum Verkauf, zu verkaufen	to save	- retten, bergen - sparen
public sale	- Auktion	saver	- Sparer(in) - Retter(in)
sales (turnover)	- Verkaufserlös, Umsatz	saving	- Sparen, Einsparen - Rettung
sales [adj]	- Verkaufs-		
salesman	- Geschäftsreisender, Verkäufer	savings	- Ersparnisse
sales promotion	- Verkaufsförderung	savings account	- Sparkonto
sales representative	- (Handels)Vertreter(in)	savings bank	- Sparkasse
saleswoman	- Verkäuferin		
to sell	- verkaufen	sense	- Sinn, Vernunft, Verständnis - Bedeutung, Ansicht
seller	- Verkäufer, Veräußerer		
selling	- Verkaufs-	to sense	- fühlen
*un*saleable	- unverkäuflich	common sense	- gesunder Menschenverstand
satisfaction	- Befriedigung - Zufriedenheit, Genugtuung	sense*less*(ly)	- sinnlos, unvernünftig, gefühllos

sense*less*ness	- Sinnlosigkeit, Unvernunft	socialization	- Sozialisierung, - Verstaatlichung, - Sozialisation
sensiblity	- Empfindungsvermögen, Sensibilität	to socialize	- vergesellschaften, - verstaatlichen, - Geselligkeit pflegen
sensible (-ibly)	- einsichtig, vernünftig		
sensitive(ly)	- empfindlich, empfindsam		
sensitivity	- Empfindlichkeit, Einfühlungsvermögen, Sensitivität	society	- Gesellschaft, Gemeinschaft
		sociology	- Soziologie
to sensitize	- (licht)empfindlich machen, sensibilisieren	to solicit	- ansuchen, werben
		solicitation	- Ansuchen
separable	- trennbar	solicited offer	- angefordertes Angebot
separate(ly)	- getrennt, gesondert	solicitor	- (Rechts)Anwalt, Anwältin
under separate cover	- mit getrennter Post		
to separate	- trennen, scheiden	solicitous	- eifrig, dienstbeflissen
separateness	- Getrenntheit, Gesondertheit	solicitude	- Besorgtheit, Dienstbeflissenheit
separation	- Trennung	*un*solicited offer	- nicht angefordertes Angebot
*in*separable (-ably)	- untrennbar		
		special(ly)	- spezial, besonders
short	- kurz, knapp	special offer	- Sonderangebot
shortage	- Fehlbetrag, Gewichtsverlust, - Verknappung, Engpaß	specialist	- Fachmann, -frau, Spezialist(in)
		specialization	- Spezialisierung
to shorten	- abkürzen, verkürzen	to specialize	- sich spezialisieren
shortfall	- Defizit	specialty	- Besonderheit, Spezialität
shorthand	- Kurzschrift, Stenographie		
to write shorthand	- stenographieren	to stabilize	- stabilisieren
shorts	- Mankoposten, - Shorts (kurze Hosen)	stabilization	- Stabilisierung
		stability	- Stabilität, Permanenz
shortsighted	- kurzsichtig	stable (stably)	- beständig, stabil, fest
short-term	- kurzfristig	*in*stability	- Unbeständigkeit, Labilität
shortweight	- Minder-(Unter-)gewicht		
skilful(ly)	- fähig, tüchtig	standard [n]	- Norm, Maßstab, Vorgabe
skill	- Fertigkeit, Fähigkeit, Kenntnis, Geschick	safety standards	- Sicherheitsbestimmungen
skilled labour, skilled manpower	- gelernte Arbeitskräfte	standard [adj]	- normal, üblich
		standardization	- Standardisierung, Vereinheitlichung
*un*skilful	- ungeschickt	to standardize	- normieren, eichen, vereinheitlichen, standardisieren
*un*skilled	- ungelernt		
sociable	- gesellig		
social(ly)	- gesellschaftlich, sozial		
socialism	- Sozialismus	subsidiary [n]	- Schwestergesellschaft, Tochtergesellschaft
socialist	- sozialistisch		
socialite	- Angehörige(r) der Oberen Zehntausend, Prominente(r)		

subsidiary [adj]	- Hilfs-, Neben-	summary [n]	- Übersicht, Darstellung
subsidy, subsidies	- Hilfsgeld, Subvention, Unterstützungsgelder	summary [adj]	- summarisch
		summation	- Addition, Summe
to subsidize	- zuschießen, subventionieren	summing-up	- Zusammenfassung
		to supervise	- beaufsichtigen
to succeed	- beerben, nachfolgen	supervising authority	- Aufsichtsbehörde
to succeed in [gerund]	- gelingen	supervision	- Aufsicht, Beaufsichtigung, Überwachung
succeeding	- nachfolgend		
success	- Erfolg	supervisor	- Aufsicht, Vorgesetzte(r)
successful(ly)	- erfolgreich	supervisory board	- Aufsichtsrat
successfulness	- guter Erfolg, Glück		
succession	- Beerbung, Nachfolge	supplier	- Lieferant, Lieferfirma
	- Reihe, Folge	supplies	- Betriebsstoffe, Hilfsstoffe
successive(ly)	- folgend		- Vorräte
successor	- (Rechts)Nachfolger(in)	to supply	- liefern, beliefern
*un*successful	- nicht erfolgreich	supply and demand	- Angebot und Nachfrage
*un*successfulness	- Erfolglosigkeit, Mißlingen	supply industry	- Zulieferindustrie
		surveillance	- Aufsicht, Überwachung
to suffice	- genügen, ausreichen	to survey	- besichtigen, prüfen
sufficiency	- Hinlänglichkeit, Angemessenheit	survey	- Übersicht
			- (Land)vermessung
sufficient	- genügend, ausreichend, hinreichend		- Untersuchung
		surveyor	- Sachverständiger(in)
sufficiently	- hinlänglich, zur Genüge		- Landvermesser(in)
*in*sufficient	- unzureichend		- Bauinspektor(in)
		suspect [n]	- Verdächtige(r)
to suggest	- vorschlagen, nahelegen	suspect [adj]	- verdächtig
suggestibility	- Beeinflußbarkeit	to suspect	- vermuten
suggestible	- beeinflußbar		- verdächtigen
suggestion	- Vorschlag, Anregung	suspected	- verdächtig
to be suggestive	- den Eindruck von etwas vermitteln	suspicion	- Verdacht
		to have a suspicion that	- den Verdacht hegen, daß
suggestively	- vielsagend, anzüglich	suspicious(ly)	- verdächtig
suggestiveness	- Zweideutigkeit, Anzüglichkeit		- argwöhnisch
		*un*suspected	- unvermutet, ungeahnt
		*un*suspicious	- unverdächtig
suit	- Anzug		
	- Klage, Prozeß	to suspend	- aufschieben, aussetzen
to suit	- passen		- aufhängen
suitable (-ably)	- geeignet, angemessen		- suspendieren
suitability	- Eignung	suspense	- Schwebe(zustand)
suitor	- Kläger(in), Prozeßpartei		- Ungewißheit, Spannung
		to keep in suspense	- in Spannung halten
*un*suitable	- ungeeignet	in suspense	- in der Schwebe
		suspension	- Aufschiebung, Suspendierung
sum	- Betrag, Summe		
to sum up	- addieren		- Schwebe-, Hänge-
to summarize	- zusammenfassen	suspension bridge	- Hängebrücke

79

technical(ly)	- technisch	transcript	- Abschrift
technical (committee)	- Fach(ausschuß)		- Niederschrift
technicality	- Detail, Formsache		- Protokoll
technician	- Techniker(in)	transcription	- siehe *transcript*
technique	- Technik, Verfahren, Methode		- Transkription
			- Umschrift, Durchschrift
technological	- technologisch		
technology	- Technologie	transfer	- Übertragung, Transfer,
			- Überweisung
theft	- Diebstahl		- Umsteigen, Wechsel
thief [pl. thieves]	- Dieb(in)	to transfer	- abtreten, transferieren,
to thieve	- stehlen		überweisen, übertragen, umbuchen
thieving [adj]	- diebisch		
thieving [n]	- Stehlen, Diebstähle		- umsteigen, wechseln
thievish	- diebisch	telegraphic transfer	- telegraphische Überweisung
thievishness	- diebische Art		
		transferable	- übertragbar
tolerable (-ably)	- erträglich, annehmbar, ziemlich	transferability	- Übertragbarkeit
		transferee	- Übernehmer(in), Erwerber(in), Zessionar
tolerance	- Toleranz, Duldsamkeit		
tolerant(ly)	- tolerant, duldsam	transference	- Überschreibung, Übertragung
to tolerate	- tolerieren, dulden		
toleration	- Tolerieren, Dulden	transferor	- Übertragende(r),
*in*tolerant	- intolerant, unduldsam		Zedent(in)
to trade	- handeln	to transmit	- senden, überbringen, übermitteln, übersenden
trade	- Gewerbe, Handwerk, Berufsgruppe		
		transmission	- (Rundfunk)Sendung, Übermittlung
	- Geschäft		
	- Warenverkehr		- Getriebe
	- Beschäftigung, Beruf	transmitter	- Sender
trade discount	- Handelsrabatt		- Übersender(in)
trade fair	- Fachmesse		
trade price	- Großhandelspreis	treat	- besondere Freude
trade unions	- Gewerkschaften	to treat	- behandeln
trademark	- Warenzeichen, Schutzmarke		- einladen zu
		treatise (on)	- Abhandlung (über)
tradename	- Firmenname	treatment	- Behandlung
trader	- Händler(in), Kaufmann, -frau	heat treatment	- Wärmebehandlung
		treaty	- Abkommen, Vertrag zwischen Staaten
tradesmen	- Gewerbetreibende, Kleinhändler		
		the Treaties of Rome	- die Römischen Verträge
trading	- Handel, handeltreibend		
		treaty of commerce	- Handelsabkommen
to transcribe	- abschreiben		
	- aufschreiben, mitschreiben	trust	- Vertrauen
			- Treuhand(schaft)
	- protokollieren		- Trust

to trust	- (stark) hoffen - (ver)trauen	trial	- Versuch, Probe - gerichtliche Untersuchung, Prozeß
trustee	- Treuhänder(in) - Bevollmächtigte(r), Vermögensverwalter(in)	on trial trial order	- auf Probe - Probeauftrag
trusteeship	- Treuhänderschaft	try	- Versuch
trustful(ly)	- vertrauensvoll	to try	- versuchen
trusting(ly)	- vertrauensvoll		- einen Fall untersuchen, verhandeln
trustworthy	- sicher, verläßlich, vertrauenswürdig	to be tried for theft	-wegen Diebstahls vor Gericht gestellt werden
trustworthiness	- Vertrauenswürdigkeit - Zuverlässigkeit	trying	- schwierig - anstrengend
*un*trustworthy	- unzuverlässig		

u

urge	- Verlangen, Bedürfnis, Drang, Trieb	use*less*(ly)	- nutzlos
		use*less*ness	- Nutzlosigkeit
to urge	- drängen, darauf dringen, eindringlich bitten	user	- Benutzer(in)
		user-friendly	- benutzerfreundlich
		*mis*use	- Mißbrauch
urgency	- Dringlichkeit	*Merke besonders:*	
urgent(ly)	- eilig, dringend	used	- gebraucht
		Used cars are much cheaper than new ones.	- Gebrauchte Autos sind viel billiger als neue.
usable	- benutzbar		
usability	- Benutzbarkeit		
usage	- Behandlung - Brauch, Sitte - Gebrauch, Anwendung	to be used to [gerund] He was used to working hard. He used to After dinner he used to smoke a cigar.	- gewöhnt sein an - Er war daran gewöhnt, schwer zu arbeiten. - er pflegte - Nach dem Essen pflegte er, eine Zigarre zu rauchen/rauchte er gewöhnlich eine Zigarre.
use	- Gebrauch, Nutzen		
to use	- benutzen		
useful	- nützlich		
usefully	- in nützlicher, brauchbarer Weise		
		Aber: he usually does	- er pflegt zu tun, er tut es gewöhnlich
usefulness	- Nützlichkeit		

valid	- bindend, gültig, rechts-gültig, in Kraft	value*less*	- wertlos
to validate	- in Kraft setzen, für rechtskräftig oder wirksam erklären	valuation	- Abschätzung, Bewertung, Würdigung
		(e)valuation	- Wertermittlung
validation	- Gültigkeitserklärung, Validierung	variable	- veränderlich, regulierbar
		variance, variation	- Abweichung, Schwankung, Veränderung
validity	- Gültigkeit, Rechtskraft		
*in*valid	- ungültig, außer Kraft	variety	- Vielfalt
to *in*validate	- außer Kraft setzen, ungültig machen	various	- verschiedene (mehrere)
		to vary	- sich verändern
*in*validation	- Kraftloserklärung, Ungültigkeitserklärung		- schwanken, variieren
*in*validity	- Ungültigkeit, Entkräftung, Invalidität	to vend	- verkaufen
		vendee	- Erwerber(in), Käufer(in)
		vending machine	- Verkaufsautomat
to valorize	- aufwerten	vendor	- Lieferant(in)
to value	- abschätzen, bewerten, taxieren, valutieren		- Verkäufer(in)
		door-to-door vendor	- Hausierer(in)
value	- Wert		
value added tax (VAT)	- Mehrwertsteuer (MWSt.)	verifiable	- nachweisbar
		verification	- Beglaubigung, Bestätigung, Prüfung
value date	- Valuta, Wertstellung		
valuable	- wertvoll	verifier	- Prüfer(in)
valuables	- Wertsachen	to verify	- prüfen, beglaubigen, nachweisen
valuer	- Taxator(in), Schätzer(in)		

Fill in the missing words:

advice – apply – benefit – carelessly – communication – competitive – complaint – concluded – consignment – consumer – convenience – correspondent – custom-made

1. The contract _____ between the agent and the principal was signed on August 5th.
2. We hope that both your company and ours will _____ from this cooperation.
3. Since then many new means of _____ have been invented.
4. Please submit an offer stating _____ prices and terms.
5. Your _____ has given cause for complaint.
6. A _____ should be lodged at once.
7. In international trade the acknowledgement of order is often replaced by an _____ of despatch.
8. Some customers of ours must _____ for an import licence before importing a machine.
9. Unfortunately our order was carried out very _____.
10. We are in a position to deliver _____ equipment for paper converting industries.
11. We would ask you to respond to our enquiry at your earliest _____.
12. Marketing capital goods is different from marketing _____ goods.
13. He intends to become a foreign language _____.

damages – decision – defective – depend – description – determined – developing – differs – distributed – diversify – division – drawee – duration

1. It goes without saying that we will send you a credit note for the _____ goods.
2. Should we suffer a loss, we shall claim _____.
3. They will further _____ their range of products.
4. You should try to contact the _____-making people of this company.
5. A detailed quotation always includes a _____ of the products offered.
6. I am _____ to improve this unpleasant situation.
7. We very much _____ on their willingness to assist us in this matter.
8. Exports to the _____ countries consist mainly of capital goods.

9 Your quotation dated September 1st _____ from the one you sent us three months ago.
10 Bills of exchange have three parties: the drawer, the _____ and the payee.
11 The _____ of his stay is scheduled for two months.
12 The profit was _____ among the partners.
13 He works for the most successful _____ of this company.

economic – effected – efficient – emphasis – employees – endorsement – entries – erroneously – estimates – exceeding – excluding – execution – exhibit – expand – expense – exposed – extent

1 The delay in the _____ of our order has caused us great inconvenience.
2 Exports have risen to some _____.
3 For orders _____ 1000 pieces we shall grant a quantity discount of 10%.
4 According to the latest _____ German firms have invested more than twenty thousand million DM in various small Asian countries.
5 The price is to be understood ex works Cologne, _____ costs for packing, freight and insurance.
6 One of the objectives of the EC is to coordinate the _____ policies of the member countries.
7 They laid special _____ on the high quality of their products.
8 At next year's Hanover Fair they will _____ some new products.
9 These parts of the machine are particularly _____ to paper dust.
10 Payment will be _____ by cheque.
11 Please return the consignment at our _____.
12 I have learnt from your advertisement in today's FAZ that you are seeking an _____ salesman.
13 We _____ invoiced 30 units instead of the 20 units we sent you.
14 On October 1st, three new _____ joined our company.
15 Our bookkeeping department made some wrong _____ and it took them several days to find the mistakes.
16 It is their firm intention to _____ even further.

facilities – fault – Fund – funds – identity – introduce – impression – invented – investments – investigate – judged – justified

1. There has been a decline in _____ within the last three months.
2. The International Monetary _____ (IMF) was established in 1945.
3. They are anxious to _____ their articles onto new markets.
4. Your complaint is not _____.
5. Please _____ this matter.
6. They have considerable _____ at their disposal.
7. They have most modern production _____.
8. An Englishman named Rowland Hill _____ the Penny Post.
9. The suspect was released after he had proved his _____.
10. I have no _____ to find with him.
11. I was under the _____ that something was wrong with him.
12. In business everybody is _____ by their success.

law – legalized – losses – maintenance – merchandise – obey – occupies – officer – omissions – operation

1. For lubrication of the machine see the attached _____ programme.
2. He did not _____ the rules.
3. The failure of a customer of ours has caused us considerable _____.
4. Errors and _____ excepted.
5. A bill becomes a _____.
6. His certificate must be _____
7. _____ is a synonym for goods.
8. The _____ of this machine is very complicated and must be simplified.
9. The police _____ told us how to get to the tourist information office.
10. Our new office _____ the whole of the third floor in this building.

permission – personal – postponed – preferred – prevented – procedure – text-processing – production – profit – promised – proprietor – prosperous – proved – provisions – publisher

1. Thin _____ margins have forced us to reduce costs wherever possible.
2. The meeting had to be _____.
3. They _____ tea to coffee.

4　His statement _____ to be true.
5　Her boss _____ her from leaving by giving her a rise.
6　The secretary had some problems with the new _____ system.
7　I enclose a _____ data sheet with details on my education and experience as a secretary.
8　Finally he found a _____ for his novel.
9　We must make _____ for doubtful debts.
10　_____ is becoming more and more automated.
11　The _____ of this block of flats had the roof repaired.
12　We must obtain his _____ to spend more money on our office equipment.
13　The goods were _____ for delivery within a fortnight.
14　It was the same _____ as every year.
15　We wish you a happy and _____ New Year.

realized – reasonable – receipt – regulations – relations – remains – repeat – stable – safe – standards – subsidiary – success – suitable – summarizing – supervision – supply – surveillance – suspect

1　It is _____ to extend the credit of this company.
2　A cheque must be presented for payment within a _____ period of time.
3　Delivery can be effected immediately after _____ of order.
4　If the quality of your articles comes up to our expectations, you may count on _____ orders.
5　The Federal Government and the Deutsche Bundesbank are responsible for keeping the currency _____.
6　Last year, they established a _____ in the United States.
7　This machine is _____ for producing paper handkerchiefs.
8　Any information you can _____ will be much appreciated.
9　We should be pleased if we could resume business _____ with your company.
10　Due to lack of money this project could not be _____.
11　They are not familiar with the German customs _____.
12　Little now _____ to be done.
13　This company is known for high quality _____.
14　His _____ is due to hard work.

15 The police questioned the _____.
16 He is responsible for the _____ of all aspects of manufacture.
17 _____ we can state that the exhibition was a great success.
18 The new airport has installed a complicated _____ system.

technicians – theft – trade – transfer – treating – treaty – trial – urgently – useful – valid

1 After carefully studying your offer we have decided to place a _____ order with you.
2 The goods have been paid for by bank _____.
3 The parts are _____ required and should be delivered by the end of this month.
4 This company badly needs some good _____.
5 The travel agency gave us some _____ information about Great Britain.
6 You may rely on our _____ your information as strictly confidential.
7 The _____ was reported to the police.
8 He has been working in this _____ for a very long time.
9 Her work permit is no longer _____.
10 A contract is concluded between companies or individuals; a _____ is concluded between states.

Translate into English:

1 Sie waren gezwungen, die Produktion einzustellen.
2 Sie drückten ihre Mißbilligung sehr deutlich aus.
3 Dieser Brief ist in einer sehr unpersönlichen und unhöflichen Art geschrieben.
4 Es ist uns leider unmöglich, Ihre Bedingungen zu akzeptieren.
5 Die starke Konkurrenz hat sie entmutigt, ihre Arbeit auf dem hiesigen Markt fortzusetzen.
6 Die Maßnahmen, die Sie ergriffen haben, sind ungeeignet, die Situation zu verbessern.
7 Die Tabelle der empfohlenen Schmierstoffe ist noch unvollständig.
8 Leider arbeitet er immer unzulänglicher.
9 Sie haben nur unzureichende Mittel zu ihrer Verfügung.
10 Die Zahlung erfolgt durch ein bestätigtes und unwiderrufliches Akkreditiv, das bei einer deutschen Bank zu eröffnen ist.
11 Die Annahmeverweigerung der Waren verursachte große Unannehmlichkeiten.
12 Wir unterscheiden zwischen angeforderten und nicht angeforderten Angeboten.
13 Seit einiger Zeit arbeitet sie sehr nachlässig.
14 Es ist nutzlos, die Angelegenheit weiter zu verfolgen.

5. Vorsicht: Fallen und Sünden

Dieses Kapitel behandelt Fallen (*traps*), in die man so leicht geht und Sünden (*sins*), die man immer wieder begeht. Es mahnt zur Vorsicht (*attention*) bei der Übersetzung bestimmter schwieriger Begriffe und Wendungen.

Vorsicht bei folgenden **englischen** Begriffen:	

to acknowledge/ acknowledgement of order
Es ist eine weitverbreitete Unsitte und falsch, von *confirmation of order* zu sprechen, wenn man die Auftragsbestätigung meint, die man aufgrund eines Auftrages schreibt oder die man auf einen Auftrag hin bekommt. Das ist *acknowledgement of order*.
We acknowledge receipt of your order dated ...
We acknowledge receipt of your letter of ...
Wollen Sie aber einen Auftrag, den Sie mündlich, also beispielsweise telefonisch erteilt haben, bestätigen, so übersetzen Sie das mit *confirm*.
We confirm our today's cable.
We confirm the order we placed with you by our today's cable.
Wenn Sie jemanden bitten, Ihnen zu bestätigen, daß er mit Ihrem Vorschlag einverstanden ist, schreiben Sie: *please confirm*.

address
Denken Sie daran, daß *address* anders geschrieben wird als die deutsche Adresse!

allowance
Allowance hat u.a. die Bedeutung von Nachlaß, der meist als Ausgleich für eine Fehlleistung oder dergleichen gewährt wird, und darf nicht mit → *discount* (Rabatt) oder → *rebate* (Bonus) verwechselt werden.
If you are prepared to accept this shipment, we shall grant you an allowance of 10 %. – Wenn Sie bereit sind, die Sendung anzunehmen, werden wir Ihnen einen Nachlaß von 10 % gewähren.

to apologize
Wenn wir uns bei jemandem entschuldigen, heißt das *apologize (for)*.
We apologize for our error/please accept our apologies. – Wir entschuldigen uns für unseren Irrtum.
Das Substantiv von *to apologize* ist *apology*.
Bitten wir den anderen, daß er entschuldigen möge, heißt es z.B. *Please excuse our error.* – Wir bitten Sie, unseren Irrtum zu entschuldigen.

to become
To become ist ein Vollverb und heißt werden, nicht etwa bekommen.
He will become a teacher. – Er wird Lehrer (werden).
Der Kellner in einem englischen Restaurant schaute den deutschen Touristen etwas verdutzt an, als dieser seine Bestellung aufgab und sagte: *"I become a steak!"*

bill

Vorsicht bei dem Wort *bill*, es kommt in verschiedenen Zusammenhängen vor:
Zunächst ist es eine Rechnung, die vorwiegend für eine erbrachte Dienstleistung ausgestellt wird, demnach im Hotel usw.
Im kaufmännischen Englisch, wo es um den Verkauf von Waren geht, schreiben wir eine *invoice*.
Außerdem bedeutet *bill* Gesetzesentwurf – *a bill becomes a law* – und es ist vielfach auch zu lesen als die Kurzform von *bill of exchange* – Wechsel. *A bill of exchange is an accepted draft*, d.h.
draft – Tratte (gezogener Wechsel)
acceptance – Akzept (Annahmevermerk)
bill of exchange – (akzeptierter Wechsel)
Merke: Im amerikanischen Englisch heißt *bill* – Geldschein.

billion

In Großbritannien ist eine Billion etwas anderes als in den USA. Zur Veranschaulichung folgendes Schema:

	deutsch	*britisch*	*USA*
1.000.000	Million	million	million
1.000.000.000	Milliarde	thousand million	billion
1.000.000.000.000	Billion	billion	trillion

Da man im Englischen da, wo wir Deutschen zur Verdeutlichung großer Zahlen einen Punkt haben, ein Komma setzt, schreiben sich dort die Zahlen wie folgt::
britisch/USA
1,000,000
1,000,000,000
1,000,000,000,000
Hinter einer ganzen Zahl, beispielsweise bei Geldbeträgen, setzt man einen Punkt, wohingegen im Deutschen ein Komma steht.
Man geht also genau umgekehrt vor: US-$ 1,800,000 aber US-$ 120.50.
Merke: 2,5% = 2.5%

to borrow

Die englischen Wörter *to borrow* und *to lend* werden oft verwechselt, weil wir im Deutschen in beiden Fällen von leihen sprechen.
to borrow – leihen
to lend – verleihen
I borrowed some money from him. – Ich lieh (borgte) mir etwas Geld von ihm.
aber: *Last year, I lent him some money.* – Letztes Jahr lieh ich ihm etwas Geld.
Es ist einleuchtend, daß *borrower* der Kreditnehmer und *lender* der Kreditgeber, der Darlehensgeber ist.

brief

Brief bedeutet im Englischen kurz, bündig.
a brief answer – eine kurze, knappe und bündige Antwort
to be mentioned briefly/ in concise form – kurz erwähnt werden
to brief somebody – jemandem genaue Anweisungen geben/jemanden instruieren. Davon kommt *briefing*, ein Gespräch, bei dem Anweisungen gegeben werden, eine Beratung über die Vorgehensweise.
A briefcase ist übrigens eine Aktentasche.

chief	*Chief* sieht dem deutschen Chef so ähnlich, ist aber nicht das, was wir im Umgangsdeutsch unter Chef verstehen. → Chef *Chiefs* gibt es bei der Polizei - *police chief* - und bei den Indianern. Sonst wird *chief* adjektivisch gebraucht und ist ein Synonym für *main*. So gibt es den *chief clerk* – Bürovorsteher(in), den *commander in chief* – oberster Befehlshaber(in), den *chief customer* – Hauptkunde, -kundin, den *Chief Justice* – Oberste(r) Richter(in).
to confirm/confirmation	→ *to acknowledge/acknowledgement of order*
consequently	*Consequently* bedeutet nicht konsequent bzw. konsequenterweise sondern folglich, infolgedessen.
dead	*Dead* gibt es auch im übertragenen Sinne, da heißt es oft völlig: *you are dead right* *dead account* – totes Konto *deadlock* – Sackgasse *The discussion reached a deadlock/ended in deadlock.* – Die Besprechung endete in einer Sackgasse. Im Kaufmännischen müssen wir außerdem wissen: *deadline* – letzte Frist, Anzeigenschluß *deadline pressure* – Termindruck
direct	*Direct* wird auch als Adverb verwendet, wenn es den Sinn von direkt, ohne Umwege hat: *Please supply direct from your factory.* *It came from overseas direct.* *The goods will be delivered direct to your address.* *We supply our goods direct from the factory* – Direktverkauf ab unserem Werk. *... taking your sales message direct to the people that count.* aber: *directly behind me* – unmittelbar hinter mir
discount	*Discount* ist Rabatt, wobei zwischen *quantity/bulk discount* – Mengenrabatt und *cash discount* – Skonto zu unterscheiden ist. Wenn man weiß, um was es geht, sagt man in beiden Fällen oft nur *discount*. *For orders exceeding 500 units we grant a quantity discount of 10 %.* – Für Aufträge von mehr als 500 Stück gewähren wir einen Mengenrabatt von 10 %. *We grant a trade discount of 25 % on our list prices.* – Wir gewähren einen Händlerrabatt von 25 % auf unsere Listenpreise. *If payment is effected within one week, we grant a cash discount of 2.5%.* – Wenn die Zahlung innerhalb einer Woche erfolgt, gewähren wir einen Skonto von 2,5 %.
to dispose of	*To dispose of* heißt zwar verfügen über, aber nicht im Sinne von haben, besitzen, sondern vielmehr in der Bedeutung von verwenden, erledigen. *The consignment has been disposed of.* – Die Sendung ist bereits verkauft/ verwendet worden.

	You may dispose of this consignment. – Sie können über diese Sendung verfügen/sie verwenden/weggeben. *to dispose of something by will* – etwas testamentarisch vermachen *to dispose of one's interest in the firm* – einen Geschäftsanteil veräußern. aber: *to have sufficient means at one's disposal* – über genügend Mittel verfügen *to hold or keep something at someone's disposal* – etwas zu jemandes Verfügung halten.
double/duplicate	Das im Kaufmännischen so oft gebrauchte „in doppelter Ausfertigung/Ausführung" (zweifach) wird nicht mit *double* sondern mit in *duplicate* übersetzt. *Please send your invoice in duplicate.* → doppelt
emigration	Verwechseln Sie nicht *emigration* – Auswanderung mit *immigration* – Einwanderung.
to excuse	→ *to apologize*
floor	*Floor* heißt neben Fußboden auch Etage, nicht aber Flur. *They live on the 2nd floor of a block of flats.* – Sie wohnen auf der 2. Etage eines Mietshauses. Vorsicht: im Amerikanischen ist das die 1. Etage, da dort *1st floor* das Erdgeschoß ist.
gift	*Gift* ist ein Geschenk (*present*) oder eine Schenkung. Das deutsche Wort Gift wird mit *poison* übersetzt. *Poisonous* ist also giftig.
heat	*Heat* kann man außer mit Hitze im Deutschen oft auch mit Wärme übersetzen. *heat accumulation* – Wärmestau *heat centre* – Wärmezentrum Im Stahlwerksbetrieb bedeutet *heat* auch Schmelzung. *heat treatment department* – Schweißerei
to ignore/to be ignorant	Beachten Sie den Unterschied zwischen dem Verb *to ignore*, das im Sinne von *to take no notice of* steht, also (jemanden) ignorieren, nicht beachten usw. heißt, und dem abgeleiteten adjektivischen Ausdruck *to be ignorant* – unwissend, ungebildet, unkundig sein, nicht kennen, nicht wissen.
immigration	→ *emigration*
information	Von *information* gibt es keine Pluralform. Ob Sie also von Information oder Informationen sprechen, es bleibt *information*. Das zugehörige Verb steht natürlich auch im Singular. *This information is brand new.* – Diese Information(en) ist/sind brandneu.
to lend	→ *to borrow*

machine tool	Wenn man jedes Wort einzeln übersetzt, ergibt sich ein Maschinenwerkzeug, also vielleicht ein Werkzeug, das man an einer Maschine benötigt. Es ist aber eine Werkzeugmaschine.
market	*To be in the market for* sagt nicht, daß man mit einem Artikel auf dem Markt ist, sondern daß man Bedarf dafür hat. *Since we are in the market for these articles, we ask you for your detailed quotation.* – Da wir diese Artikel benötigen/ Bedarf für diese Artikel haben, bitten wir um Ihr ausführliches Angebot.
measure/measurement/ to measure	*Measure* bedeutet Maß (Abmessung) und Maßnahme. *Litres are a more convenient measure than pints.* – Ein Liter ist ein besseres Maß als ein Pint. *Measurement is the result of measuring something, e.g. I did not measure the door correctly and gave the wrong measurements to the carpenter.* – Ich habe die Tür nicht richtig abgemessen und dem Schreiner die falschen Abmessungen angegeben. *to take measures (steps)* – Maßnahmen ergreifen
milliard	*Milliard* gibt es nur im britischen Englisch → *billion*.
million	→ *billion*
news	*News* ist insofern tückisch, als es zwar ein *s* hat, aber doch immer ein Singularbegriff bleibt. *I have good news for you.* – Ich habe eine gute Nachricht/gute Nachrichten für Dich. *No news is good news!*
to notice/notice	Es sieht aus wie die deutsche Notiz, bedeutet aber bemerken bzw. Bemerkung. Die Bemerkung im Sinne von Anmerkung dagegen ist *remark*. Mit *notice* gibt es im Kaufmännischen einige wichtige Ausdrücke: *to give notice* – kündigen *to terminate without prior notice* – mit sofortiger Wirkung beenden (lösen) *until further notice* – bis auf Widerruf
to pay (for)	Die Präposition macht den Unterschied in der Bedeutung. *to pay for the meal* – die Mahlzeit bezahlen *to pay the bill* – die Rechnung bezahlen
people	*People* hat nie ein *s*, wenn es sich um Leute handelt. *Peoples* sind Völker. *the people in India* – die Leute in Indien *the peoples of Asia* – die Völker Asiens.
principally	*Principally* ist ein Synonym von *mainly* und *chiefly* und heißt nicht prinzipiell. Verwechseln Sie nicht *principal* und *principle*: *He acted against his principles.* – Er handelte gegen seine Prinzipien. *He acted against his principals.* – Er handelte gegen seine Chefs.

probe	*Probe* ist nicht Probe im Sinne von Muster (*sample*), sondern Sonde (medizinisch und technisch) Außerdem kann es auch Untersuchung im Sinne von *investigation* heißen. → Probe (Seite 20)
to prove	*To prove* heißt nicht prüfen, sondern beweisen, sich erweisen usw. Das Substantiv ist *proof*. → prüfen (Seite 21)
public	*Public* bedeutet öffentlich und Öffentlichkeit. Vorsicht bei dem Begriff *public school*, wobei es sich um eine britische Privatschule, wie beispielsweise Eton, handelt.
rebate	*Rebate* ist kein Rabatt, sondern ein Bonus, d.h. eine nachträglich gewährte Vergütung. So kann der Lieferant dem Kunden bei Erreichen einer bestimmten Bestellmenge am Ende des Jahres einen Bonus – *a rebate* gewähren, oder eine Fachzeitschrift, in der eine Firma im Laufe des Jahres die für einen Bonus erforderliche Anzahl Anzeigen aufgegeben hat, gewährt bei der Abrechnung einen Bonus.
regulation	*Regulation* ist eine Vorschrift, eine Satzung, eine Dienstordnung oder dergleichen, keine Regulierung im Sinne einer Schadensregulierung. Eine solche Regulierung ist *adjustment*.
to remember/to remind (of)	Es ist zu unterscheiden zwischen: *to remember* – sich selbst erinnern *to remind someone of* – jemand an etwas erinnern *Do you remember our first meeting?* – Erinnern Sie sich an unser erstes Treffen? *May we remind you of our invoice of ...* – Dürfen wir Sie an unsere Rechnung vom ... erinnern. Erinnern kann man auch anders übersetzen: *to recall a name* – sich an einen Namen erinnern *What does Trafalgar Square commemorate?* – Woran erinnert Trafalgar Square?
some	*Some* als Adverb bedeutet ungefähr, etwa: *There were some hundred visitors.* – Es waren etwa hundert Besucher dort. aber: *There were some hundreds of visitors.* – Es waren einige Hunderte von Besuchern dort.
soon	*Soon* ist ein Adverb und heißt bald. Das deutsche Adjektiv baldig kann also nicht mit *soon* übersetzt werden. *We expect you to answer soon.* – Wir erwarten, daß Sie bald antworten. *We are looking forward to your early reply.* – Wir sehen Ihrer baldigen Antwort gerne entgegen.

United States	Die Vereinigten Staaten werden als vereinte Nation gesehen, und es heißt deshalb *the United States is*. Entsprechend ist das Personalpronomen *it* oder *she* und das Possessivpronomen *its* oder *her* zu setzen. Übrigens, wenn der Engländer von seiner Nation spricht, sagt er immer *her*, also *England and her history*.

Vorsicht bei folgenden **deutschen** Begriffen:

auch	Kommt auch in einem ganzen Satz vor, wird es mit *also, too, as well* oder *equally* übersetzt: *She also works very hard. I am also tired.* *He has a house of his own, too.* *I, too, am very tired.* *She is tired as well.* *I am equally tired* (gleichermaßen). Sagt man aber nur kurz "ich auch", d.h. man hat im Deutschen keinen vollständigen Satz, so muß man sich im Englischen auf den vorhergehenden Satz beziehen und sagen: *I'm tired. So am I.* *I can help him. So can I.* *I work very hard. So do I.* Das heißt: Steht im ersten Satz ein Hilfsverb, so bildet man „ich auch" mit diesem Hilfsverb. Steht im ersten Satz ein Vollverb, so bildet man „ich auch" mit der entsprechenden Zeit von *to do*. Dasselbe trifft für den verneinenden Ausdruck „ich auch nicht" zu. Hier benötigt man das Wort *neither*: *I'm not tired. Neither am I.* *I can't help him. Neither can I.* *I don't work very hard. Neither do I.*
Ausstellung/Messe	Im Kaufmännischen meinen wir mit Ausstellung oft die Messe. Das ist *exhibition* oder *fair* (*Hanover Fair, Leipzig Fair*). Im Amerikanischen wird eher *exposition* verwendet. Man spricht auch von *show*. Ausstellungs-/Messegelände – *exhibition ground* Messeveranstalter – *organizers of an exhibition* Ein Ausstellungsraum beispielsweise einer Firma ist *showroom*. Die Auslage von Waren ist *display*.
bald/baldig	→ *soon*
bestätigen/Bestätigung	→ *to acknowledge/acknowledgement*
Billion	→ *billion*
Bonus	→ *rebate*

Chef

Chef mit *chief* zu übersetzen, ist falsch. Das ist *boss*. Sprechen wir vom höchsten Chef, ist das der *Managing Director* oder der *General Manager*.

dauern

Dauern heißt zwar *to last*, aber oft wird es anders übersetzt:
Es wird einige Wochen dauern, bis die Sendung ankommt. – *It will take a few weeks until the consignment arrives.*
Es dauerte einige Stunden, bis ich es ihm erklärt hatte. – *It took me some hours to explain it to him.*
aber: *The strike will last three weeks.*

Doppel-/Doppel/doppelt

Nicht alle diese Begriffe werden mit *double* übersetzt. Unterscheide:
Doppelbuchstabe – *double letter*
Doppelfenster – *double window*
Doppel (Duplikat) – *duplicate*
Doppel (Kopie) – *copy*
Doppel im Tennis – *doubles*
in doppelter/zweifacher Ausfertigung – *in duplicate*
eine doppelte/zweifache Quittung/Empfangsbescheinigung – *a duplicate receipt*
doppelseitig – *two-sided*
doppelstöckig – *two-storey, twin-storey*
Merke:
Doppelbett – *double bed*
zwei Betten – *twin beds*

entschuldigen

→ *to apologize (for)/apologies*

erinnern

→ *to remember/to remind (of)*

Hilfe

Das einfachste Wort für Hilfe ist *help*, aber im kaufmännischen oder wirtschaftlichen Englisch ist es oft besser, von *assistance* zu sprechen.
We thank you in advance for your kind assistance in this matter. – Wir danken Ihnen im voraus für Ihre freundliche Hilfe (Unterstützung) in dieser Angelegenheit.
Zusammengesetzte Wörter mit Hilfe werden in vielen Fällen mit dem alleine kaum vorkommenden *aid* übersetzt:
Entwicklungshilfe – *development aid*
Wirtschaftshilfe – *economical aid*
Militärhilfe – *military aid*
Auslandshilfe – *foreign aid*
erste Hilfe – *first aid*

immer

Vorsicht bei der Übersetzung von immer! *Always* ist nur richtig, wenn immer die Bedeutung von immer wieder, immer wiederkehrend usw. hat.
Er kommt immer zu spät. – *He always comes late.*
aber:
Sie wird immer bekannter. – *She is getting more and more popular.*
Die Stadt wird immer größer. – *The town grows bigger and bigger.*
Um dieses immer auszudrücken, wiederholt man also den Komparativ des Adjektivs.

Es gibt weitere Möglichkeiten, immer auszudrücken:
Er warnt uns immer wieder. – *He keeps warning us.*
Das macht es uns immer schwieriger. – *That makes it increasingly difficult for us.*

leihen, verleihen	→ *to borrow*
Messe	→ *Ausstellung*
Milliarde	→ *billion*
Million	→ *billion*
Nachlaß	→ *allowance*
Notiz	Eine Notiz, die man jemanden macht oder hinlegt, ist nicht *notice*, sondern *note*. Eine Aktennotiz ist ein *memo* (von *memorandum*), Plural *memos*.
Politik	Die "große" Politik wird mit *politics* übersetzt. Wenn es aber um die beispielsweise in einem Unternehmen verfolgte Politik geht, um die Richtlinien, die man dort hat, spricht man von *policy*. Handelspolitik – *trade policy* Preispolitik – *price policy* Währungspolitik – *monetary policy*
prinzipiell	Prinzipiell (im Prinzip, grundsätzlich, an sich) heißt *in/on principle, for reasons of principle*, nicht aber *principally*. → *principally*
Rabatt	→ *discount* → *allowance* → *rebate*
Regulierung	Auf eine Beschwerde, Mängelrüge – *complaint* hat eine Regulierung zu folgen. Das ist im Englischen *adjustment*, nicht *regulation*.
spät	Wenn wir sagen, daß er zu spät kam, heißt das einfach: *He was late.*
Übersee	Hier nicht das *s* am Ende vergessen; demnach Überseeländer – *overseas countries* Überseegebiete – *overseas territories* Überseegeschäft, -handel – *overseas trade*
ungefähr	*about* (nicht abkürzen) *approximate (ly) - approx.* Auch *some* heißt manchmal ungefähr. → *some* Ungefähr, etwa mit den informellen Ausdrücken *roughly* oder *in the neighbourhood/region of* zu übersetzen, ist bei Lieferzeitangaben falsch.
Unternehmer	Sagen Sie nicht *undertaker*, das heißt Leichenbestatter.

	Je nach Anwendung ist Unternehmer: *entrepreneur, employer* – Arbeitgeber, *industrialist* – Industrieller/Großunternehmer, *manufacturer* – Hersteller.
während	Verwechseln Sie nicht *during* und *while*! Während unseres Aufenthaltes in London ... – *During our stay in London ... (during + noun)* Während wir uns in London aufhielten/in London waren ... – *While we were staying in London ... (while + verb)*
Wechsel	Der Wechsel, das Zahlungsmittel, ist *bill of exchange*, oft auch kurz *bill* genannt. Ein noch nicht akzeptierter Wechsel, eine Tratte, dagegen ist *draft*.
Werbung	Das Wort Werbung spielt im Kaufmännischen eine große Rolle. Im allgemeinen handelt es sich um *advertising*, nicht zu verwechseln mit *advertisement* (auch *advert* und *ad*), eine Werbeanzeige oder Annonce in der Zeitung oder Fachzeitschrift. Also: *the costs for advertising were too high.* Ein Werbebrief ist ein *sales letter*, also kein *advertising letter*. Für die Werbung gibt es auch andere Ausdrücke, z.B. *publicity, promotion*. Bei der Fernsehwerbung spricht man von einem *commercial*. Merke: Werbekampagne – *publicity campaign* Verkaufsförderung – *sales promotion*
Woche	Wenn wir im Deutschen 8 Tage sagen, sagt der Engländer *one week*; der Begriff 14 Tage kann nicht wörtlich übersetzt werden. Es heißt *in two weeks/in a fortnight*. Die 1., 2., 36. Woche usw. wird übersetzt: *the week commencing January, September ...*

Translate into English:

1. Bitte schicken Sie uns Ihre Auftragsbestätigung sobald wie möglich zu und geben Sie darin die kürzest mögliche Lieferzeit an.
2. Sie zieht es vor, Krankenschwester zu werden.
3. Alle Informationen werden streng vertraulich behandelt.
4. Hast du die Notiz gelesen, die sie für dich hinterlassen hat?
5. Es hat sich als vorteilhaft erwiesen, neue Mitarbeiter gründlich zu schulen.
6. Es ist empfehlenswert, einen Vertreter in einem überseeischen Land zu haben, da er mit allen dortigen Bestimmungen vertraut ist.
7. Die Vereinigten Staaten sind eine relativ junge Nation.
8. Die Regierung wird sich damit beschäftigen müssen, ob die Entwicklungshilfe erhöht werden kann.
9. Wir müssen darauf bestehen, daß Sie uns einen Nachlaß auf den Gesamtbetrag Ihrer Rechnung vom 21. Februar gewähren.
10. Was gedenken Sie zu tun, um unsere Beschwerde zu regulieren?
11. Die Lieferung wird etwa im 3. Quartal des nächsten Jahres erfolgen.
12. Ein Wechsel kann diskontiert und verlängert werden.
13. Sie ist in diesem Unternehmen für die Verkaufsförderung verantwortlich und hat eine interessante Tätigkeit.
14. In etwa 8 Tagen wird Herr Müller aus seinem Urlaub zurück sein. Er wird sich dann umgehend an Sie wenden.
15. Unser Besuch wird in der 10. Woche erfolgen.

Übersetzen Sie ins Deutsche:

1. We should like to settle this matter amicably, and we therefore offer you an allowance of 10%.
2. In order to facilitate introduction of the products onto the English market, we shall grant you a discount of 15%.
3. They have the most modern machine tools.
4. As you have placed a total of 12 advertisements in the course of last year, we shall grant you the promised rebate of 5% on all current invoices.
5. We remember the time we spent with you in Germany with great pleasure.
6. We regularly visit the most important fairs both in Germany and abroad.
7. Please excuse our failure to arrange your hotel accommodation.
8. Our day-to-day work is becoming increasingly more difficult and hectic.
9. The reform of Community farm policy was slow.
10. In principle we agree to this arrangement; there are only some slight amendments which must be discussed.
11. These cases are destined for overseas and must be marked as such.
12. An entrepreneur/employer has to take many risks.
13. Sales letters must be written with particular care.
14. May we remind you of the fact that payment of our invoice of February 25th amounting to £850 is overdue. Please remit this amount to one of our accounts.

6. Vorsicht auch bei der Orthographie!

Nachstehend finden Sie eine Reihe gleichklingender und nahezu gleichklingender Begriffe, die Sie nebeneinander sehen sollten, um sich die Unterschiede in der Schreibweise zu merken. Da man im Deutschen die weichen Vokale b, d und g oft hart, nämlich als p, t und k, spricht, werden auch die im Englischen eigentlich deutlichen Unterschiede oft nicht beachtet. Die Auflistung enthält auch ähnlich aussehende Wörter, die Fehlerquellen darstellen.

a

accept/except	annehmen/ausnehmen, außer
access/excess	Zugang/Übermaß
advice/advise	Rat/raten, informieren
affect/effect	beeinträchtigen, Affekt/bewirken, Wirkung
ambassador/ embassy	Botschafter/Botschaft
angle/angel	Winkel/Engel

b

bag/back	Tasche, Beutel/zurück, Rücken
belief/believe	Glaube/glauben
blade/plate	Klinge/ Platte
bloc/block (Sterling bloc)	Block politisch/Block allgemein
born/borne	geboren/getragen (von *to bear*)
break/brake	brechen, Pause/bremsen, Bremse

c

calf/carve	Kalb, Wade/schnitzen
cease/seize	aufhören/ergreifen
class/glass	Klasse/Glas
clause/close	Klausel/schließen, Schluß
college/colleague	College/Kollege, Kollegin
complimentary/ complementary	Gruß-/zusätzlich (*the complimentary close of a letter*)
confectionary/ confectionery	Konfektions-/Konfekt, Zuckerwerk

co-operation/ corporation	Zusammenarbeit/Körperschaft, Handelsgesellschaft,
council/counsel	Ratsversammlung, Körperschaft von Ratgebern/Beratung, Rechtsbeistand
course/cause	Lauf, Kurs/verursachen, Ursache
cross/gross	Kreuz, kreuzen/brutto

d

dear/deer	liebe (r), sehr geehrte (r)/Rotwild
degree/decree	Grad, akadem. Grad, Ausmaß/Erlaß, Dekret
device/devise	Vor-, Einrichtung, Gerät/ersinnen, ausdenken, vererben (Grundstücke)

e

effect/affect	bewirken, Wirkung/beeinträchtigen, Affekt
embassy/ ambassador	Botschaft/Botschafter
emigration/ immigration	Auswanderung/ Einwanderung
ensure/insure	garantieren/versichern
except/accept	ausnehmen, außer/annehmen
excess/access	Übermaß/Zugang
expand/expend	ausdehnen/ausgeben (Geld)
extend/extent	ausdehnen/Ausmaß

f

face/faith	Gesicht, gegenüberstehen/ Glaube
fair/fare	fair, Messe/Fahrgeld
feed/feet	füttern/Füße, Fuß als Maß
few/view	wenige/Ansicht, Aussicht
fir/fur	Tanne, Fichte/Pelz
flower/flour	Blume/Mehl
food/foot	Nahrung/Fuß
formerly/ formally	früher/formell, förmlich

g

glass/class	Glas/Klasse
graze/grace	weiden, grasen/Anmut, Anstand (*Your Grace* - Euer Gnaden)
gross/cross	brutto/Kreuz, kreuzen
guild/guilt	Gilde/Schuld

h

high/height	hoch/Höhe
hole/whole	Loch/ganz

i

immigration/ emigration	Einwanderung/ Auswanderung
insure/ensure	versichern/garantieren
intend/intent/ indent	beabsichtigen/Absicht/ Vertrag(surkunde), Auslandsauftrag, einrücken, Einzug
it's/its	*it is* oder *has*/sein, ihr, sein

j

joined/joint	beigetreten, zusammengefügt/gemeinsam (*joint venture*)

l

lag/leg/lack	nachhinken, Verzögerung/ Bein/fehlen, Mangel
lie/lay	liegen, sich selbst legen/ setzen, stellen, legen
leaf/leave	Blatt/verlassen, Urlaub
letter/latter	Brief/letztere(r)
lose/loose	verlieren/lose

m

mail/male	Post/männlich
meet/meat	begegnen/Fleisch
merry/marry	fröhlich/heiraten

p

passed/past	Vergangenheit von *to pass*/ Vergangenheit, vorbei
peace/piece/peas	Frieden/Stück/Erbsen
personal/ personnel	persönlich/Personal
plane/plain	glätten, Flugzeug, Ebene/ einfach, schlicht, Ebene
plate/blade	Platte/Klinge
position/ possession	Lage, Position/Besitz
precede/proceed	vorausgehen/fortfahren, fortsetzen
price/prize	Preis (einer Ware)/Preis, Auszeichnung
principle/ principal	Prinzip, Grundregel/Dienstherr(in), Auftraggeber(in), hauptsächlich
prove/proof	beweisen, sich erweisen/ Beweis, Nachweis, Probeabzug

q

quiet/quite	ruhig/ganz

r

rent/rend (rent, rent)	Miete, Riß, Spaltung/spalten, bersten
rely (on)/relay	sich verlassen auf/Relais
ride/rite/right	reiten, fahren, Ritt, Fahrt/Ritus/richtig
rise/raise	steigen, aufgehen/erheben, steigern
role/roll	Rolle, die man spielt/rollen, Rolle
robe/rope	Gewand, Robe/Seil
root/rude	Wurzel/grob, unflätig

s

safe/save	sicher/retten, sparen
sale/sail	Verkauf/segeln, Segel
seize/cease	ergreifen/aufhören
seam/seem	Naht/scheinen
serious/series	ernst, schwerwiegend/Reihe, Folge
sight/site/side	Sicht/Gelände/Seite
slide/slight	gleiten, Schieber, Dia/geringfügig
speak/speech	sprechen/Rede
stare/stair	starren/Treppe
stationary/ stationery	stationär, fest/Schreibpapier, -waren

steal/steel	stehlen/Stahl
staff/stuff	Personal/Sachen, stopfen

t

tale/tail	Erzählung, Bericht/Schwanz, Ende
than/then	als (beim Komparativ)/dann, danach
there/their	dort/ihre
treat/tread	behandeln/treten, schreiten

v

view/few	Sicht/wenige

w

wander/wonder	bummeln, herumirren/ Wunder, sich wundern
weak/week	schwach/Woche
weather/whether	Wetter/ob
which/witch	welche(r,s), der, die, das/Hexe
whole/hole	ganz/Loch

Setzen Sie den oder die fehlenden Buchstaben ein:

1. Unfortunately, we cannot ___ept your offer.
2. I urgently need your advi___e.
3. Your name was given us by the German ___mbassy in Madrid.
4. The managers always travel first ___lass.
5. She has a strong belie___ in delegation.
6. Private housebuilding s___ms to have peaked this year.
7. Prices have been f___ly stable.
8. Last year there was a sl___t rise in mortgage rates.
9. The princip___ and traditional functions of commercial banks are to accept deposits and to supply industry with circulating capital in the form of short-term loans.
10. Twelve countries have join___ the EC.
11. The drawee accepts a draft by writing his name across the f___ of the bill.
12. The new Stock Exchange account opened in qui___ a depressed mood yesterday.
13. Dissolution of a partnership may also be ___ffected by a de___ree of the court.

14 A c___poration is a legal entity.
15 If your articles m___t our requirements, we shall place a substantial order with you.
16 Delivery of the goods can be ___ffected in about two weeks.
17 We must win back old customers who have c___sed placing orders with us.
18 An offer is firm unless it contains a cl___se to the contrary.
19 The range of th___ products includes Scottish Tweeds.
20 Please, indicate length, width and h___ght of the machine.
21 We can offer both a station___ry and a portable version of this unit.
22 It helps me sa___ a lot of time and money.
23 We are also in a po___ion to supply more th___n the quantity ordered.
24 Many support the former alternative, but I personally favour the l___tter.
25 Before making a decision as to w___ther we will place an order with you, we ask to arrange for a sample to be sent to us.
26 Unless we can offer our goods at more favourable prices, we will l___se customers.
27 The prices for meals are qu___ reasonable there.
28 She wanted to see some of the s___s of London before she continued her journey to Leeds.
29 They enjoyed their r___e on the bus very much.
30 When he caught s___t of her, he shouted in a loud voice.
31 Big Ben is very d___r to most English people.
32 I w___der whether goods are more expensive in England th___n in Germany.
33 The Queen regularly receives ___bassadors and other diplomatic representatives.
34 The importance of the House of Lords has diminished increasingly in the c___se of time.
35 In Germany tennis has been playing a predominant r___ for some years now.
36 The ties between the Commonwealth countries have become l___ser and l___ser.
37 In his election campaigns, Kennedy pleaded for p___ce and equal rights for all citizens.
38 We can now advi___e you that the consignment was shipped by rail this morning.
39 Your c___peration in this matter would be much appreciated.
40 On the occasion of that meeting he was awarded the pri___e.
41 The goods have to be packed carefully to ___sure sa___e arrival.
42 Please let us know whether ___ross and net weights are to be stencilled on the cases.
43 A receipt is a pr___ of payment.
44 We have no hesitation in granting them credit to the exten___ you mentioned.
45 They have done business with us for the pa___ two years.
46 The delays in the execution of our orders are c___sing us great inconvenience.
47 Your information was pa___ on to our customers.
48 We are afraid that all this will have ser___s consequences for our company.
49 We shall do our utmost to m___t this deadline.
50 Owing to bad w___ther the vessel could not s___.
51 They form___ly invited us for dinner.
52 All his st___ff were dismissed, because he closed down his business.
53 The br___es on your car must be repaired immediately.
54 As agreed upon, ___surance will be covered by you.
55 All boys and girls of the class pa___ the examination, ___ept him.
56 We belie___ you will never find a better one.
57 We build machines and equipment for the chocolate and confection___ry industry.
58 This envelope machine can be equipped with a dev___e for producing pockets.
59 For the pa___ twenty years I have been employed by Smithe and Horton.
60 They seek to r___se their standard of living.
61 He delivered a most interesting sp___ch.
62 Please l___ the book on my desk. The book l___s on my desk.

7. Abkürzungen

Wie in allen Sprachen, so gibt es auch im Englischen eine große Anzahl Abkürzungen. Nachstehend eine Sammlung der *abbreviations*, die in der Wirtschafts- und Korrespondenz-Sprache am häufigsten benötigt werden.

a

a.a.r. *against all risks* — Versicherung gegen alle Gefahren
A.C., a.c. *alternating current* — Wechselstrom
a.m. *ante meridiem* — vormittags
a/m *above mentioned* — oben erwähnt
ad *advert advertisement* — Anzeige
A/P *account purchases* — Abrechnung des Einkaufskommissionärs
A/S *account sales* — Verkaufsabrechnung bei einem *consignee* - Konsignator

b

BC *Before Christ* — vor Christus
B.E. (B/E) *bill of exchange* — Wechsel
B.L. (B/L) *bill of lading* — Konossement
BOTB *British Overseas Trade Board* — staatliche britische Außenhandelsförderungsstelle

c

C *centigrade* — Celsius
c.a.d. *cash against documents* — Kasse gegen Dokumente
CAD *computer-aided design* — computergestützte Konstruktion
CAM *computer-aided manufacture* — computergestützte Fabrikation
c.b.d. *cash before delivery* — Zahlung vor Lieferung
cc *cubic centimetre* — Kubikzentimeter
c.& f. *cost and freight* — Kosten und Fracht
c.& i. *cost and insurance* — Kosten und Versicherung
C/I *certificate of insurance* — Versicherungszertifikat
C.I.A. *cash payment in advance* — Vorauszahlung
c.i.f. *cost, insurance, freight* — Kosten, Versicherung und Fracht
c.i.f.& c. *cost, insurance, freight and commission* — Kosten, Versicherung, Fracht und Provision
c.i.f.& i. *cost, insurance, freight and interest* — Kosten, Versicherung, Fracht und Zinsen
c.i.f.c. & i. *cost, insurance, freight, commission and interest* — Kosten, Versicherung, Fracht, Provision und Zinsen
CIO *Congress of Industrial Organizations* — Gewerkschaftsbund (USA)

C.K.D./CKD
  completely knocked down — völlig zerlegt (bei Versand), *a CKD kit* – ein Bausatz
COBOL *Common Business Oriented Language* — problemorientierte Programmiersprache
c.o.d./COD *cash on delivery* — per Nachnahme
C/F carr.fwd. *freight forward* — unfrei, Empfänger zahlt Fracht
C/P carr.pa *freight (pre)paid* — frachtfrei
c.o.s. *cash on shipment* — Zahlung bei Verschiffung
C.P.A. *certified public accountant* — Wirtschaftsprüfer(in)
CT *cable transfer* — telegraphische Auszahlung
CTP *Community Transit Procedure* — gemeinschaftliches Versandverfahren, innerhalb der EG
cu.ft. *cubic foot, cubic feet* — Kubikfuß
CWO *cash with order* — Zahlung bei Auftragserteilung

d

D/A *documents against acceptance; documents accepted; deposit account* — Dokumente gegen Akzept; Annahme; Sparkonto
db/DB/dB *decibel* — Dezibel
D.C./d.c. *direct current* — Gleichstrom
D/D *documentary draft* — Dokumententratte, Rembourswechsel
D/P *documents against payment, cash against documents* — Dokumente gegen Kasse, Dokumente gegen bar
...d/s *...days' sight* — ...Tage Sicht
DTP *desktop publishing* — Desktop publishing
dwt *tons deadweight* — Tragfähigkeit

e

EC *European Community* — Europäische Gemeinschaft (EG)
EDP *electronic data processing* — elektronische Datenverarbeitung (EDV)
E+E *errors excepted* — Irrtum vorbehalten
E+OE *errors and omissions excepted* — ausgenommen evtl. Irrtümer und Auslassungen
EFTA *European Free Trade Association* — Europäische Freihandelsvereinigung
e. g. *for example (exempli gratia)* — zum Beispiel
E.O.M. *end of month, e.g. 2/10 E.O.M.* — 2 % Skonto für Zahlung innerhalb 10 Tagen nach dem Ende des Liefermonats
EPU *European Payments Union* — Europäische Zahlungsunion
ERM *exchange rate mechanism* — Wechselkursmechanismus
EURATOM *European Atomic Energy Community* — Europäische Atomgemeinschaft

f

F *Fahrenheit*	Fahrenheit
f *foot, feet*	Fuß
f.a.q. *fair average quality*	Durchschnittsqualität
f.a.s./ F.A.S. *free alongside ship*	frei längsseits Schiff
frt.fwd. *freight forward*	Fracht nachzunehmen
frt.pp. *freight prepaid*	Fracht vorausbezahlt
FCR *Forwarding Agent's Certificate of Receipt*	Spediteurübernahmebescheinigung
F.I.C.A. *Federal Insurance Contribution Act*	Gesetz über Abgaben zur Sozialversicherung (USA)
F.I.T. *Federal Income Tax*	Bundeseinkommensteuer (USA)
FTC *Federal Trade Commission*	Bundesbehörde zur Verhinderung monopolistischer oder wettbewerbseinschränkender Praktiken (USA)
FOA *free of average*	frei von Havarie
f.o.b./F.O.B. *free on board*	frei Schiff
f.o.c. *free of charge*	kostenfrei
f.o.q. *free on quai*	frei Kai
f.o.r. *free on rail*	frei Waggon
f.o.s. *free on ship*	frei Schiff
f.o.t. *free on truck*	frei Waggon

g

GA *general average*	große, gemeinschaftliche Havarie
GATT *General Agreement on Tariffs and Trade*	Allgemeines Zoll- und Handelsabkommen
GDP *gross domestic product*	Bruttosozialprodukt
GMT *Greenwich Mean Time*	Westeuropäische Zeit
GNP *gross national product*	Bruttosozialprodukt

h

HD *heavy duty*	Hochleistungs-...
e.g. HD oil	z.B. Hochleistungsöl
HGV *heavy goods vehicle*	LKW
H.M. *His/Her Majesty's*	Seine/Ihre Majestät

i

IATA *International Air Transport Association*	internationaler Verband der Luftfahrtgesellschaften
i/c, I/C *in charge*	vom Dienst
ICC *International Chamber of Commerce*	Internationale Handelskammer

ICFTU *International Con-*
  federation of Free Trade Unions internationaler Bund freier Gewerkschaften
ID *Immediate Delivery* Auftrag auf Abfertigung zur sofortigen Auslieferung
I.D. (card) *identity card* Ausweispapier
i. e. *that is (id est)* das heißt
inst. *instant* dieses Monats (veraltet)
IMF *International Monetary Fund* Internationaler Währungsfonds
IOU *I owe you* Schuldschein
IRC *International Reply Coupon* internationaler Antwortschein
ISBN *International*
  Standard Book Number internationale Standard-Buch-Nummer
IT *information technology* Informationstechnik

k

K *thousand, e. g. She earns 15 k.* -tausend, z. B. Sie verdient 15 000.
kgs *kilogram(me)s* Kilos

l

lb(s) *pound(s)* Pfund = 453,49 Gramm
L/C *Letter of Credit* Akkreditiv
LCL *less than carload lot* (US) Stückgut
LPM *lines per minute* Linien pro Minute
Ltd. *limited company* Kapitalgesellschaft in Großbritannien
Merke: Es gibt die private *limited company* – etwa die deutsche GmbH oder Familien-AG – und die *public limited company.* Im letzteren Falle werden die *shares* – Anteile, Aktien – öffentlich gehandelt. In Australien, Hong Kong, Singapur, etc und in Südafrika heißen die *limited companies* übrigens *proprietory limited company* – **Pty.Ltd.**

m

MD *managing director* Geschäftsführer(in)
M/P *months after payment* Monate nach Zahlung
...m/s *...months' sight* ...Monate Sicht
M.R. *mate's receipt* Verladebescheinigung, Empfangsquittung einer Ladung
MS *motorship* Motorschiff
MT *mail transfer* briefliche Auszahlung
MV *motor vessel* Motorschiff

n

n/a *not applicable* entfällt
n.f.o. *new for old* neu für alt (bei Versicherung)
N/T *new terms* neue Bedingungen
n.wt. *net weight* Nettogewicht

o

o/a	*on or about*	am oder ungefähr (beim Datum)
OAS	*organization of American States*	Organisation der Amerikanischen Staaten
OECD	*Organisation for Economic Cooperation and Development*	Organisation für wirtschaftliche Zusammenarbeit und Entwicklung
O.P.	*open policy*	offene Police (Versicherung)
OSHA	*Occupational and Safety Health Administration*	amerikanische Berufsgenossenschaft: Sicherheit und Gesundheit am Arbeitsplatz
O/T	*old terms*	alte Bedingungen
oz	*ounce(s)*	Unze(n) - 28,35 Gramm

p

PA	*personal assistant; public address (system)*	persönliche(r) Referent(in); Lautsprecheranlage
P/A	*power of attorney*	Generalvollmacht
P.A.	*particular average*	besondere Havarie
p&p	*postage and packing*	Porto und Verpackung
PAYE	*Pay As You Earn*	Lohnsteuer [GB]
p.c.	*per cent*	v. Hundert, Prozent
pd.	*paid*	bezahlt
p/i	*proforma invoice*	Proformarechnung
Pl	*place*	Platz (in Adressen)
Plc	*public limited compamy*	Aktiengesellschaft [GB]
p.m.	*post meridiem*	nachmittags
PO	*post office; postal order*	Postamt; Postanweisung
P.O.D.	*payment on delivery*	zahlbar bei Ablieferung
ppd.	*prepaid*	vorausbezahlt
PR	*public relations*	Öffentlichkeitsarbeit, Public Relations
prox.	*proximo*	nächsten Monats (veraltet)
P.S.	*postcript*	Nachsatz
p.t.o.	*please turn over*	bitte wenden
Pty.Ltd.	*proprietory limited company*	Kapitalgesellschaft in Australien, Hong Kong, Singapur, etc und Südafrika

r

RC	*Roman Catholic*	römisch-katholisch
Rd	*Road*	Straße (in Adressen)
R&D	*research and development*	Forschung und Entwicklung
rect/ rept	*receipt*	Quittung
R.O.G.	*receipt of goods, e.g. 2/10 R.O.G.*	2 % Skonto für Zahlung innerhalb 10 Tagen nach Erhalt der Waren
RP	*reply paid*	Rückantwort bezahlt
RPM	*resale price maintenance*	vertikale Preisbindung
r.p.m.	*revolutions per minute*	Umdrehungen pro Minute

s

S.(sgd) *signature, signed* — gezeichnet, unterzeichnet
S.D.B.L. *sight draft and bill of lading enclosed* — Sichtwechsel und Konossement beigeschlossen
SEATO *South-East Asia Treaty Organization* — Süd-Ost-Asien-Pakt
SS *steamship* — Dampfer
sq.yd(s) *square yard(s)* — Quadratyard

t

t.l.o. *total loss only* — nur gegen Totalverlust
TM *trademark* — Warenzeichen
TT *telegraphic transfer* — telegrafische Auszahlung
TU *trade union* — Gewerkschaft
TUC *Trade Union Congress* — Gewerkschaftsbund [GB]

u

ult. *ultimo* — letzten Monats (veraltet)
u.t. *usual terms* — gewöhnliche Bedingungen

v

VAT *value added tax* — Mehrwertsteuer (MWSt.)
VDU *visual display unit* — Datensichtgerät
viz. *namely* — nämlich
vs *versus* — gegen (eine Partei gegen eine andere)

w

w/e *week ending ...* — Woche von ... bis ...
w.g. *weight guaranteed* — garantiertes Gewicht
w/o *without* — ohne
w/m *weight or measure* — Gewicht oder Maß
wp *wordprocessor* — Textverarbeitungssystem
wpm *words per minute* — Wörter pro Minute (Schreibmaschine)
W.R. *war risk* — Kriegsrisiko
wt *weight* — Gewicht

y

yd(s) *yard(s)* — Yard

8. Präpositionen

Es kann wohl keiner von sich behaupten, er beherrsche die englischen Präpositionen voll und ganz! Sie bereiten immer wieder einmal Probleme, insbesondere deshalb, weil sie sich in vielen Ausdrücken nicht mit den entsprechenden deutschen Präpositionen (Verhältniswörtern) decken. Sich verlassen auf heißt zwar zufällig *to rely on*, aber z.B. bei dem Ausdruck interessiert sein an muß man schon wissen, daß die Präposition unterschiedlich ist und es *to be interested in* heißt. Das bedeutet also, daß man grundsätzlich alle Verben und Ausdrücke mit den dazugehörigen Präpositionen lernen muß.

In diesem Kapitel wird der Komplex Präpositionen nach vier unterschiedlichen Gesichtspunkten behandelt:
1. Die wichtigsten Präpositionen und ihre Bedeutungen
2. Präpositionen und Partikel in Verbindung mit Verben
3. Deutsche und englische Präpositionen im Vergleich
4. Besonderheiten

1. Die wichtigsten Präpositionen und ihre Bedeutungen

about bedeutet **umher** und **über** (letzteres in Ausdrücken). *About* kann auch ein Adverb sein; dann bedeutet es **überall**, **ringsum**, **herum** und **ungefähr**.
to travel about the world
to worry about
somewhere about here
to run about
at about 8 o'clock

above → over

after heißt **nach** in einem zeitlichen Zusammenhang und wenn man von der Reihenfolge spricht. Dann kann es auch **hinter** heißen.
after breakfast
the day after tomorrow – übermorgen
to arrive one after another – nacheinander ankommen
after all – schließlich
Merke: *to be dressed after the latest fashion* – nach der letzten Mode gekleidet sein
Nach im Sinne von **gemäß** übersetzt man im kaufmännischen Englisch mit *according to* oder *as per*: *according to your order*
as per the list we sent you.

at bezieht sich hauptsächlich auf einen Punkt, entweder zeitlich oder örtlich
at that moment
at 8 o'clock
at his house
Merke: *to be at school/church* – in der Schule/Kirche sein
to be at university – an der Universität sein
to have lunch at a restaurant – im Restaurant essen *(not at home)*

Außerdem kann *at* sich noch auf Preise oder Umstände beziehen:
at £2 a kilo
at 5p per mile
to be good at something
to be at peace

amid(st) heißt **inmitten** oder bildlich auch **bei**.

among(st) heißt **unter** oder **zwischen**:
among friends
He distributed his money amongst the poor.
a village among the hills

before/behind *before* ist **vor**, zeitlich und eingeschränkt auch örtlich, *behind* ist **hinter**, örtlich:
before his birthday
before his eyes
before a committee
behind the house
Als Adverb heißt *before* **früher, zuvor**.

below → *under*

beside heißt örtlich **neben**, bildlich bedeutet es **außerhalb, außer, neben**:
He was beside himself with excitement. – Er war außer sich vor Aufregung.

besides dagegen ist sowohl Präposition als auch Adverb. Als Präposition heißt es **außer**, als Adverb **außerdem, ferner, weiterhin**; es hat also hier die Bedeutung von *furthermore* bzw. *moreover*.

between **zwischen** ist nur richtig, wenn es **zwischen zwei** bedeutet.
He is sitting between his sisters.
Aber: *There was one employee among* (zwischen/unter) *them who could not be relied on.*
There was one rose amidst (nur eine Pflanze dieser Gattung) *all the tulips.*

beyond heißt als Präposition **jenseits**:
beyond the lake
oder **nach, über ... hinaus**:
beyond next month
Es wird in zahlreichen Ausdrücken im übertragenen Sinne verwendet:
beyond our control – außerhalb unserer Kontrolle, unseres Einflusses
beyond recovery – unheilbar krank

by Vorsicht mit *by*: es kann nur selten mit dem deutschen **bei** übersetzt werden. Ausdrücke, die in diesem Zusammenhang zu merken sind, finden Sie ab Seite 119. Hier wird die Bedeutung der Präposition *by* in ihrem eigentlichen Sinn behandelt.
by bedeutet **mittels, durch**; es steht in erster Linie beim Passiv, wo es im Deutschen **von, durch** heißt.
The letter was written by his secretary.

Die Bedeutung von **mittels** und **durch** hat *by* auch in Sätzen, die mit dem Gerundium gebildet werden.
He earns his money by translating English books.
He earns his money by translations.
You will learn these words by repeating them over and over again.
Man tut sich oft schwer mit der Übersetzung solcher Sätze ins Deutsche, da man dort einen Nebensatz bilden muß. In vielen Fällen kann man einen guten deutschen Satz bilden, wenn man den Nebensatz mit **indem** einleitet.
Seine Bedeutung von **mittels**, **durch** bestätigt das Wort *by* auch in den Begriffen, die eine Beförderung mit einem Verkehrsmittel ausdrücken.
by airmail
by airfreight
by bus
by car
by rail – mit der Bahn
by underground etc.
Ausdrücke, die im Deutschen keine Präposition haben, sind z.B.
by the hour – stundenweise
by the kilo – kiloweise

down → *up*

for heißt zunächst einmal **für**, aber es hat eine ganze Reihe anderer Bedeutungen:
He comes for dinner. – zu (Ziel, Zweck, Absicht)
I can't see for the fog. – wegen des Nebels
to be known for – bekannt sein wegen
to be famous for – berühmt sein wegen
for fear of – aus Furcht vor
to stay for a week – eine Woche lang bleiben
She has been playing tennis for many years. – Sie spielt seit vielen Jahren Tennis.
We walked for miles. – Wir sind meilenweit gegangen.
Besonders wichtig auch: *for* nach einem Komma bedeutet **denn**, **nämlich**:
Where could you get a better knowledge of international commerce and finance than in the heart of that world, England, for, believe me, England is still the heart of it!

from *from ... to...* – von ... bis ...
örtlich und zeitlich:
from Munich to Cologne
from eight to nine o'clock
von ... ausgehend/kommend:
from my point of view
to die from hunger

in/into, on/onto *in* antwortet auf die Frage wo? (Dativ)
into antwortet auf die Frage wohin? (Akkusativ)
I am in the room. – Wo bin ich?
I go into the room. – Wohin gehe ich?

Diese Regel kann man auf *on* und *onto* übertragen.
He is on the roof. – Wo ist er?
He climbs onto the roof. – Wohin klettert er?
Zeitlich gesehen bedeutet *in* **in** oder **innerhalb**:
in 1991 – im Jahre 1991
I see you in three weeks. – Ich sehe Sie in drei Wochen.
in the first four years – innerhalb der ersten vier Jahre
Merke: *on* kommt von der älteren Form *upon*; daher kommen Ausdrücke wie z.B.
as agreed upon – wie vereinbart.

of   **von** dient zur Bildung des Genitivs:
In the course of the day.
A cup of coffee.
Merke: anstelle *the car of his father – his father's car* (sächsischer Genitiv)

off   heißt als Präposition **von** im Sinne von **weg** bei Bewegung bzw. Entfernung:
She jumped off the roof.

out/out of   heißt als Präposition **aus, aus ... heraus**
to go out the window
Do not lean out of the window!

over/above   *over* (**über**) ist das Gegenteil von *under* (**unter**)
above (**oberhalb**) das Gegenteil von *below* (**unterhalb**):
He is going over the road.
The bridge over the Rhine.
The bedroom is above the dining room.
The plane is flying above the clouds.
The details mentioned above.
Bei *above* sollte man also an **oberhalb** denken, obwohl man im Deutschen oft nur **oben** sagt.
Hierhin gehört auch der deutsche Begriff **obige**, den wir für **oben genannt** sagen:
The above mentioned firm.
Merke: *He is over 21 years old.*
It took me over 5 hours.
He is above any criticism.
That is above me.
Over als Adverb heißt **darüber**, *above* als Adverb heißt **oben**.

since   in Verbindung mit einem Zeitpunkt bedeutet **seit**:
In Germany, we have had peace since 1945.
I have not seen him since our recent visit to Great Britain.
Merke: seit mit einem Zeitraum ist *for*:
In Germany, we have had peace for almost 50 years now.
I have not seen him for about half a year.

till/until   Diese beiden Wörter stehen für das zeitliche **bis**:
We will be here till 9 o'clock.
Until 1945, we had war in Germany.

through	ist **durch**, räumlich und bildlich: *The burglar entered the house through the window.* *To handle a market through an agency.* *A disturbance through a fault in the electric system.* Merke: *through France* – durch Frankreich *throughout France* – durch ganz/überall in Frankreich
to	heißt **zu**, **nach**: *to go to England,* *they went to church* In zeitlichen Zusammenhängen heißt es **vor**: *three minutes to eight* Es dient außerdem zur Bildung des Dativs *to him* – ihm, *to her* – ihr und des Infinitivs. Es kann einen Zweck ausdrücken: *I did it to help him.*
toward(s)	heißt **zu, in Richtung auf, in Beziehung auf, gegen**: *We walked towards the next town.* *Her feelings towards him.* *towards eight o'clock*
under/below	*under* (**unter**) ist das Gegenteil von *over* (**über**) *below* (**unterhalb**) ist das Gegenteil von *above* (**oberhalb**) *The carpet lies under the table.* *The cat came from under the bed.* *It is under there.* *Munich is below Cologne.* *He is below him (in rank).* *10 degrees below zero.* *Just below the knee.* Bei *below* sollte man also an **unterhalb** denken, obwohl wir im Deutschen oft nur **unten** sagen: *The company mentioned below.* *Under* als Adverb heißt **darunter**, *below* als Adverb heißt **unten**.
up/down	*up* und *down* heißen als Präpositionen **oben, hinauf** und **unten, hinunter** *further up/down* *to go up/down the street*
via	heißt als Präposition **über** in Sätzen wie: *He is travelling via London to Oxford.* *via airmail* = *by airmail*

2. Präpositionen und Partikel in Verbindung mit Verben

Die Aufstellung erhebt keinen Anspruch auf Vollständigkeit. Wenn die verschiedenen Präpositionen bei einem Verb mit der ursprünglichen Bedeutung der Präposition übereinstimmen und deshalb keine Schwierigkeiten erwartet werden, oder wenn Ausdrücke für die Wirtschaftssprache nicht oder weniger relevant sind, wurde auf die Aufnahme der entsprechenden Ausdrücke verzichtet. In manchen Fällen handelt es sich in der Liste nicht um Präpositionen sondern um Adverbien. Diese wurden aufgenommen, um eine größere Übersicht zu geben.

to agree with	zustimmen, einer Meinung sein mit
to agree to	zustimmen: *He agreed to our suggestion.*
to agree on	sich einigen, übereinkommen: *They agreed on a contract.*
to apply	anwenden, auftragen
to apply for	sich bewerben um, beantragen: *They applied for an import licence/a job/ a loan etc.*
to apply to	sich beziehen auf: *The same applies to.* = *The same is true for.*
to call	rufen, anrufen
to call at	vorbeigehen bei
to call for	rufen nach; erfordern
to call off	absagen
to call on	besuchen
to call up	einberufen
to carry	tragen, befördern
to carry forward	eine Zwischensumme vortragen
to carry on	weiterführen: *to carry on business*
to carry out	ausführen: *Repairs or orders are carried out.*
to carry over	vortragen
to carry through	durchführen: *An arbitration was carried through.*
to close	schließen, beenden
to close down	schließen, zumachen, stillegen
to close in	anbrechen, hereinbrechen: *The evening was closing in.*
to close in on	einholen, sich jemandem nähern: *The police were closing in on the murderer.*
to close off	absperren
to close up	ab-/zuschließen, zumachen; zusammenrücken
to close with	(handels)einig werden mit
to come	kommen, ankommen
to come about	passieren
to come across	treffen auf
to come for	kommen wegen
to come through	durchkommen, überstehen

to cut	schneiden, unterbrechen, abbrechen
to cut down	einschränken: *to cut down on smoking*
to cut in	sich einschalten
to cut off	abschneiden, abstellen
to deal in	handeln mit, etwas verkaufen
to deal out	austeilen: *to deal out justice*
to deal with	sich beschäftigen mit
to draw	ziehen, zeichnen
to draw in	anziehen: *to draw in a crowd*
	He was drawn in on the project.
to draw off	losfahren
to draw on somebody	einen Wechsel auf jemanden ziehen
to draw up	aufsetzen: *The agreement/contract was drawn up.*
to embark for	sich einschiffen nach
to embark in/on	sich auf etwas einlassen
to enter	betreten, eintreten
to enter into	eintreten in: *They entered into negotiations.*
to enter upon	sich einlassen auf; beginnen: *She entered upon her new career with trepidation.*
to enter up	eintragen
to fall	fallen
to fall behind	zurückbleiben
to fall behind with	in Rückstand geraten
to fall for	hereinfallen auf
to fall in	einstürzen
to fall off	zurückgehen, abnehmen
to get	bekommen, werden
to get along/on	zurechtkommen, vorankommen, auskommen
to get back to	zurückkommen auf
to get into	geraten: *You always get into difficulties.*
to get off	aus-/absteigen: *Get off the bus at the next stop.*
to get on	einsteigen in
to get through	durchkommen
to get up	aufstehen
to go	gehen, laufen, funktionieren (bei Gerät)
to go ahead	vorangehen: *She went ahead and did it.*
to go beyond	hinausgehen über
to go by	vorbeigehen
to go into	sich mit etwas befassen: *The boss is going into that matter.*
to go up	steigen

to hold	halten, festhalten
to hold against	übelnehmen: *Don't hold that against her, it's not her fault.*
to hold back	zögern, unterlassen
to hold down	niedrig halten: *We succeeded in holding the costs down.*
to hold off from	sich fernhalten von
to hold on	warten
to hold to	festhalten an
to hold up	verzögern
to keep	halten, behalten, unterhalten
to keep at	weitermachen
to keep away (from)	nicht näher herankommen (an): *Danger! Keep away from wires.*
to keep back	zurückbleiben
to keep down	niedrig halten
to keep from	abhalten von
to keep off (from)	sich fernhalten (von)
to keep on	weitermachen
to keep out	draußen bleiben
to keep to	sich halten an: *Turn right, then keep to the main road.*
to look	schauen
to look after	sich kümmern um: *They looked after our interests.*
to look ahead	bevorstehen
to look around	umherschauen
to look at	schauen auf
to look back	sich umschauen, zurückblicken
to look for	suchen: *He looked for a new job/a secretary.*
to look forward to	entgegensehen, sich freuen auf: *We are looking forward to hearing from you soon.*
to look into	prüfen, nachgehen (einer Sache)
to look through	durchsehen
to look up	hochschauen, aufblicken
to look up	besuchen, aufsuchen: *Look me up when you are in town.*
to look upset	verstört schauen
to operate	arbeiten, funktionieren, tätig sein
to operate on	einwirken auf jemand oder etwas
to operate on a person	jemanden operieren
to pass	reichen; verbringen; vergeben; einbringen: *to pass a bill*
to pass along	vorbeigehen
to pass away	fortgehen, sterben
to pass beyond	darüber hinausgehen
to pass by	vorübergehen
to pass down	weitergeben, vererben
to pass for	gelten, gehalten werden für: *She is older but she passes for twenty.*

to pass into	übergehen in
to pass on	weitergeben
to pass out	ohnmächtig werden
to pass over	(stillschweigend) übergehen, unbeachtet lassen
to pass through	durchgehen, durchreisen
to pass under	sich unterziehen
to pay	bezahlen
to pay by	mit etwas bezahlen: *Can I pay by credit card?*
to pay for	etwas bezahlen
to pay in	einzahlen
to pay in cash	bar bezahlen
to pay off	abbezahlen: *The car is almost paid off.*
to pay up	zurückzahlen, bezahlen
to put	setzen, stellen, legen
to put forward	vorbringen, vorschlagen, vorlegen
to put off	verschieben, ablenken: *Don't put the appointment off again.*
to put on	anziehen
to put through	durchbringen; durchmachen lassen; (am Telefon) verbinden: *to put a bill through*
to run	laufen, fahren, führen: *She runs the business.*
to run into	treffen auf
to run out	zuende gehen; ablaufen: *The contract has run out.*
to run out off	(bald) nicht mehr haben: *We've run out of paper for the printer.*
to run up	machen: *She's run up debts of £700.00.*
to run up against	stoßen auf: *He never expected to run up against such difficulties.*
to see	sehen, verstehen
to see off	jemanden verabschieden
to see to	sich kümmern um
to seek	suchen
to seek after	verfolgen, begehren
to seek for	suchen/trachten nach
to seek out	ausfindig machen
to set	setzen, stellen, legen, festlegen
to set about	sich an etwas machen
to set against	gegenüberstellen: *Her story was set against his and nobody believed her.*
to set apart	beiseite stellen; unterscheiden
to set aside	beiseite setzen; abschaffen
to set down	absetzen; niederschreiben
to set forth	darlegen, hervorheben, erläutern
to set off	abreisen; losgehen lassen; hervorheben, zur Geltung bringen
to set on	hetzen auf: *If you don't pay they'll set the bailiffs on you.*
to set up	aufstellen; ein Geschäft eröffnen: *She set up business on her own.*

to settle	besiedeln; entscheiden; erledigen: *The invoice was settled.*
to settle down	zur Ruhe kommen, sich eingewöhnen
to settle for	sich zufrieden geben mit
to settle in	sich niederlassen in: *They settled in North America.*
to settle on (upon)	sich entscheiden für
to stay	bleiben
to stay at	wohnen in: *That's a nice hotel to stay at.*
to stay away	wegbleiben
to stay behind	zurückbleiben
to stay in	zuhause bleiben; wohnen in, leben: *I don't want to go out, let's stay in.*
to stay off	ausbleiben; wegbleiben von
to stay on	noch bleiben
to stay out	draußen bleiben: *She never manages to stay out of trouble.*
to take	nehmen
to take back	zurücknehmen; zurückbringen: *I take back what I said, it was silly.*
to take off	starten, abfliegen; entfernen, abnehmen
to take on	annehmen, übernehmen; antreten gegen: *In this position one has to take on a lot of responsibility.*
to take over	übernehmen: *She took over her sister's business.*
to take up	aufgreifen: *The boss took up most of his suggestions.*
to talk	sprechen, reden
to talk about	reden über
to talk at	einreden auf
to talk back	(frech) antworten: *Don't talk back at your boss!*
to talk of	reden von
to talk on	weiterreden
to talk out	ausdiskutieren
to talk over	bereden, besprechen: *Let's talk this over in peace and quiet.*
to talk round	herumreden um; umstimmen: *She talked everybody round to seeing it her way.*
to talk to (with)	reden mit: *Have you talked to/with him yet?*
to turn	drehen
to turn about	sich umdrehen; umkehren
to turn against	sich wenden gegen: *Everybody turned against him when he said they would have to cut three hundred jobs.*
to turn off	ausdrehen, ausmachen
to turn on	anstellen
to turn out	sich herausstellen: *It turned out that she was a personal computer specialist.*
to turn up	erscheinen, auftauchen
to wonder	sich fragen, gerne wissen mögen: *We wonder whether this matter can be settled to our satisfaction.*
to wonder at	sich wundern über: *They wonder at his patience.*

to write	schreiben
to write down	aufzeichnen, notieren
to write in	eintragen, einfügen
to write off	(schnell) herunterschreiben; abschreiben: *He wrote off bad debts. You can write that car off, it can't be repaired.*
to write up	aufschreiben; ausführlich beschreiben; schreiben über: *Who is writing up the minutes? He's writing up the film for the local newspaper.*

3. Deutsche und englische Präpositionen im Vergleich

Vorsicht bei **bei** und *by*:	bei Abfahrt – *on departure*
	bei Ankunft – *on arrival*
	bei näherer Betrachtung – *on closer inspection*
	bei Erhalt – *on receipt*
	bei Fälligkeit (z.B. eines Wechsels) – *at maturity*
	bei dieser Gelegenheit – *on this occasion*
	bei der ersten Gelegenheit – *at the first opportunity*
	Zahlung bei Lieferung – *cash on delivery*
	bei Rückkehr – *on return, on returning*
	bei Vorlage – *on presentation*
	bei einer Person wohnen – *to live with a person*
	in der Nähe von München wohnen – *to live near Munich*
	zahlbar bei der ... Bank – *payable at ... Bank*
	beim ersten Versuch – *on the first attempt*
	by the fireside – am Kamin
	by the same post – mit gleicher Post
	by the name of – namens
	by the end of this month – bis (spätestens) Ende dieses Monats
	we promise delivery by... – wir versprechen die Lieferung bis ...
	by 10 % – um 10 %
	the prices were increased by 10 % – die Preise wurden um 10 % erhöht
	by all means – selbstverständlich
	by means of – mittels
	by no means – keinesfalls
	by the way – übrigens
Schwierig können auch **an**, **am** und **auf** sein:	früh am Morgen – *early in the morning*
	am 21. Mai – *on May 21st*
	am Rhein – *on the Rhine*
	am Telefon – *on the phone*
	Interesse an – *interest in*
	reich sein an – *to be rich in*
	leiden an – *to suffer from*
	eine Antwort auf – *an answer to*
	blind sein auf (dem rechten Auge) – *to be blind in (the right eye)*
	auf Kosten von – *at the expense of*
	schätzen auf – *to estimate/value at*
	auf der Straße – *in the street/on the road*

In und **im** werden häufig mit *on* übersetzt:	im Alter von – *at the age of* im Dienst – *on duty* im Durchschnitt – *on an average* im Gegenteil – *on the contrary* im großen und ganzen – *on the whole* im ersten Stock des Hauses – *on the first floor of the house* in seinem Gesicht – *on his face* in hohem Grade/Maße – *to a great extent*
Mit wird zwar oft mit *with* übersetzt, aber nicht immer:	mit Absicht – *on purpose* mit anderen Worten – *in other words* mit leiser Stimme sprechen – *to speak in a low voice* mit jemandem verheiratet sein – *to be married to somebody* mit zehn multiplizieren – *to multiply by ten*
Wenn **nach** nicht zeitlich ist, gibt es viele Übersetzungsmöglichkeiten:	beurteilt werden nach (seinen Taten) – *to be judged by (his actions/deeds)* zu urteilen nach (seinem Akzent) – *to judge from (his accent)* nach meinem Geschmack – *to my taste* meiner Meinung nach – *in my opinion*
Unter übersetzt man häufig mit *on*:	unter diesen Bedingungen – *on these conditions* unter der Bedingung, daß – *on condition that* unter diesen Umständen – *under these circumstances*
Vorsicht bei **von**:	beim Genitiv und beim Datum ist es *of*, beim Passiv ist es *by*, aber: von etwas leben – *to live on* von etwas sprechen – *to talk about*
Zu hat viele Übersetzungen, nicht nur *to*:	zu Fuß – *on foot* gratulieren zu – *to congratulate on* zu Ihren Gunsten – *in your favour* Das paßt nicht zu blau. – *That doesn't go with blue.* zu jeder Zeit – *at any time* zu unserer Zufriedenheit – *to our satisfaction*

4. Besonderheiten

at – in – with	Achten Sie auf folgende Unterschiede: *to be good at* – gut sein in *to be weak in* – schwach sein in *He was good at English and weak in playing tennis.* *to be weak with somebody* – nachsichtig gegen jemanden sein
at – on	Merke besonders die folgenden Ausdrücke mit *at* und *on*: *We deliver at prices and on terms!* *The machine was quoted at (the price of) £1,000.* *We are prepared to deliver on the terms stated in our quotation.*

to refer to	In der Handelskorrespondenz hat dieser Begriff zwei Bedeutungen: *We refer to your letter of* ... – Wir beziehen uns auf Ihren Brief vom ... *The company has been referred to us.* – Die Firma ist an uns verwiesen worden.
to meet	Es gibt *to meet* mit und ohne Präposition: *to meet (a person)* – treffen, begegnen *We will meet you at the station.* – Wir werden Sie am Bahnhof abholen. *to meet a demand* – einer Forderung nachkommen *to meet the wishes/ requirements of* – den Wünschen/Anforderungen nachkommen/gerecht werden *to meet with approval* – Zustimmung finden
in time – on time	Beachten Sie den Unterschied: *in time* – rechtzeitig *on time (punctually)* – pünktlich *We will inform you in (due) time.* *The goods must be delivered on time (punctually).*

Es gibt Verben, zu denen im Deutschen eine Präposition gehört, im Englischen aber nicht. Dazu gehören **appoint** (ernennen zu), **elect** (wählen zu), **proclaim** (ausrufen als) und **consider** (ansehen als).
   He was appointed sole agent. – Er wurde zum Alleinvertreter ernannt.
   He was elected chairman. – Er wurde zum Vorsitzenden gewählt.
   aber: *He was elected to the Senate.* – Er wurde in den Senat gewählt.
   He was proclaimed winner. – Er wurde als Sieger ausgerufen.
   He was considered (to be) a rich man. – Er wurde als reicher Mann angesehen.
   aber: *He was regarded as a rich man.*

im Moment	Viele Fehler werden bei der Übersetzung des deutschen Begriffs **im Moment** gemacht. Gewöhnlich heißt es: *at the moment* (*at* für Zeitpunkt) aber: *He is occupied for the moment.* (Das oft verwendete *in the moment* ist in jedem Falle falsch!)
pro	Im Deutschen können wir sagen 50 km in der Stunde, 50 km die Stunde, 50 km pro Stunde. Im Englischen heißt es: *50 kilometres an hour* Vergleiche: *once a month* *twice a day* *three times a year*
Problem	In der kaufmännischen Korrespondenz geht es oft um die Lösung von Problemen. Merke: *to find a solution to a problem* – die Lösung eines Problems/für ein Problem finden *to solve a problem* - ein Problem lösen

Fill in the missing prepositions:

1. Three years ago, we entered _____ negotiations _____ this supplier, but we have not yet come _____ terms.
2. I cannot agree _____ your suggestion to deliver the goods one month later, because these spare parts are urgently needed.
3. They applied _____ the import licence, but so far it has not yet been granted _____ the authorities.
4. They have been dealing _____ this matter _____ quite a long time.
5. We have drawn _____ you for the amount _____ our invoice dated December 1st.
6. He will have lunch _____ a restaurant, because it would take him too long _____ come home.
7. The _____ mentioned order covers 10 different articles.
8. Acts _____ God are _____ our control.
9. The letter _____ recommendation was written _____ his secretary.
10. Please forward the consignment _____ airfreight.
11. Apart _____ two days at Christmas, Mr Steed has not had a day off _____ ten months.
12. You will have all amenities _____ your disposal.
13. Be careful _____ the road!
14. He stayed _____ his parents _____ three hours.
15. First they had a look _____ Buckingham Palace.
16. He is not as good _____ cricket as his brother.
17. For an order _____ 100 units and more we are prepared to grant you a quantity discount _____ 15%.
18. The goods you have ordered will be delivered subject _____ our usual terms and conditions.
19. We hope that this order will be executed _____ the end of this month.
20. Essen and its surroundings are rich _____ coal.
21. Charles is a student _____ the University of Oxford.
22. Most parents are proud _____ their children.
23. Electric light came _____ use _____ the end of the 19th century.
24. Let us have a look _____ the scenes.
25. I know her only _____ name.
26. When does the next train leave _____ Cologne?

27 _____ my opinion your parents are wrong.
28 If the articles meet _____ our customers' approval, you may count _____ substantial orders from us.
29 Please look _____ the matter and let us have your comments _____ your earliest convenience.
30 We are looking forward _____ your reply _____ great interest.
31 The goods have been delivered except _____ item 0231 which is out _____ stock.
32 He is not interested _____ his father's business.
33 The poor old lady had to live _____ very little money.
34 Our present management is quite different _____ what it was.
35 _____ the past ten years our working conditions and our wages have improved considerably.
36 I am _____ a loss how to assist you _____ this matter.
37 My principal is away _____ business; he will not be back _____ Monday.
38 The articles will be paid _____ _____ cheque.
39 She is eagerly waiting _____ the doctor who has been operating _____ her husband _____ three hours now.
40 Increase _____ production is our most important objective _____ the coming year.
41 We are looking _____ an agent who has experience _____ the North American market.
42 Please find enclosed our invoice amounting _____ £998.
43 We refer _____ your recent inquiry.
44 They came across many difficulties which they did not know how _____ solve.
45 He used to live _____ his means.
46 We regret having to inform you that a decision has been made in favour _____ your competitors.

9. Britisches und amerikanisches Englisch

In diesem Kapitel betrachten wir britisches und amerikanisches Englisch unter drei verschiedenen Gesichtspunkten:

1. Unterschiedliche Schreibweise im Englischen
2. Unterschiedliche Schreibweise im britischen und amerikanischen Englisch
3. Unterschiedliche Wörter im britischen und amerikanischen Englisch für deutsche Begriffe

1. Unterschiedliche Schreibweise im Englischen

Es gibt oft die Möglichkeit, ein Wort auf unterschiedliche Weise zu schreiben. In diesen Fällen sollte man sich aber innerhalb eines Schriftstückes unbedingt einheitlich für die eine oder die andere Version entscheiden. Im Amerikanischen wird nur die mit [US] gekennzeichnete Form verwendet.

centigramme [selten]	**centigram** [US]	Zentigramm
to despatch	**to dispatch** [US]	versenden, verschicken
despatch	**dispatch** [US]	Versand, Versendung
to enquire	**to inquire** [US]	anfragen
enquiry	**inquiry** [US]	Anfrage
to endorse	**to indorse** [US]	indossieren, weitergeben
endorsee	**indorsee** [US]	Indossat
endorsement	**indorsement** [US]	Indossament
endorser	**indorser** [US]	Indossant, Girant
kilogramme	**kilogram** [US]	Kilogramm
programme	**program** [US]	Programm
waggon	**wagon** [US]	Fracht-, Last- oder Rollwagen

Diagram und **telegram** werden auch im Englischen immer mit einem m geschrieben.

2. Unterschiedliche Schreibweise im britischen und amerikanischen Englisch

britisch	amerikanisch	
align	aline	ausrichten
calibre	caliber	Kaliber, Eigenschaft, Gehalt, Wert
catalogue	catalog	Katalog
centilitre	centiliter	Zentiliter
centimetre	centimeter	Zentimeter
centre	center	Mittelpunkt
cheque	check	Scheck
colour	color	Farbe
defence	defense	Verteidigung

britisch	amerikanisch	
favour	favor	Gunst, Gefallen
flavour	flavor	Duft, Aroma
fibre	fiber	Faser, Fiber
gauge	gage	Lehre (zum Einstellen)
harbour	harbor	Hafen
honour	honor	Ehre
humour	humor	Humor
labour	labor	Arbeit, Arbeitskräfte
licence	license	Lizenz
metre	meter	Meter; merke: *Meßinstrument* = *meter* in beiden Fällen
mould	mold	Form
offence	offense	Angriff
storey	story	Stockwerk, Etage
theatre	theater	Theater
traveller	traveler	Reisende(r)
tyre	tire	Reifen am Auto
whisky	whiskey	Whisky; merke: nur das Getränk, das in den USA gebrannt wird, heißt *whiskey*; ein importiertes Getränk ist auch dort ein *whisky*, e.g. *Scotch Whisky*

3. Unterschiedliche Wörter im britischen und amerikanischen Englisch für deutsche Begriffe

britisch	amerikanisch	
litter bin	trash/garbage can	Abfalleimer (auf der Straße)
(Public) Limited Company	Stock Corporation	Aktiengesellschaft
lift	elevator	Aufzug
(credit) enquiry agency	commercial/mercantile agency	Auskunftsbüro
staff shares	employee stock	Belegschaftsaktien
petrol	gas	Benzin
letterbox	mailbox	Briefkasten
wallet	billfold	Brieftasche
postman, -woman	mailman, -woman	Briefträger(in)
pavement	sideway	Bürgersteig
quilt	comforter	Deckbett; Steppdecke
first floor	second floor	1. Etage
inflammable	flammable	feuergefährdet
driving licence	driver's license/permit	Führerschein
pedestrian crossing	crosswalk	Fußgängerüberweg
General Manager, Managing Director	President, Chief Executive Officer	Generaldirektor(in), Vorstandsvorsitzende(r)
luggage	baggage	Gepäck
shop	store	Geschäft
credit/debit note	credit/debit memo(randum)	Gutschrifts/Lastschriftsanzeige
small luggage	handbaggage/carry-on baggage	Handgepäck
handbag	purse	Handtasche

britisch	amerikanisch	
autumn	**fall**	Herbst
wood wool	**excelsior**	Holzwolle
estate agent	**realtor**	Immobilienmakler(in)
cinema	**movie theater**	Kino
(luggage) boot	**trunk**	Kofferraum
lorry [selten **truck**]	**truck**	Lastwagen
queue	**line**	Menschenschlange
thousand million	**billion**	Milliarde
rubbish	**garbage**	Müll
postal code	**zip code**	Postleitzahl
Poste Restante, General Delivery	**To be called for**	postlagernd
bill	**check**	Rechnung (im Gasthaus/Hotel)
lawyer	**attorney**	Rechtsanwalt, -anwältin
reception	**check-in**	Empfang, Rezeption
tights	**pantyhose**	Strumpfhose
petrol station	**gas station**	Tankstelle
taxi	**cab**	Taxi
on second thoughts	**on second thought**	bei näherer Überlegung
underground	**subway**	Untergrundbahn
vest	**undershirt**	Unterhemd
curtains	**drapes**	Vorhänge
(water) tap	**(water) faucet**	Wasserhahn
waistcoat	**vest**	Weste
works manager	**plant manager**	Werksleiter
flat	**apartment**	Wohnung

Schlüssel zu den Übungen

Kapitel 1

Translate into English:

I 1 They refused acceptance of the consignment./They rejected the consignment.
   2 The design of the machine was modified and it now runs much better.
   3 These import restrictions must be/will have to be abolished.
   4 The order cannot be executed/carried out punctually/on time.
   5 There is sufficient labour in this region.
   6 This matter will be handled most carefully.
   7 Your enquiry (inquiry) has been treated confidentially/as strictly confidential.
   8 Our representative will visit you within/in the next two weeks/fortnight.
   9 It must be emphasized/stressed that we will not assume any responsibility in this matter.
   10 The printing press offered by you is more expensive than that of your competitors.

II 1 All these factors will have an impact on our country's economy.
   2 Some of our new articles were introduced onto the North American market.
   3 Production of such articles will be discontinued.
   4 The goods delivered do not come up to your samples.
   5 We shall/will do our utmost/our best to comply with your wishes.
   6 The government of this country is constantly trying to raise the standard of living of the poor.
   7 By mistake you were sent an invoice for (the) parts which were to be delivered free of charge.
   8 The suspect was questioned by the police.
   9 There are four vacancies in our company at the moment.
   10 He has conducted/run his business with great success for more than 20 years now.

III 1 We should take appropriate measures to lower our prices in order to be more competitive.
    2 We promise to despatch (dispatch) the goods in exactly three days, i.e. on June 1st.
    3 The average return/yield/profit is most satisfactory.
    4 The price is to be understood free border.
    5 There is a considerable demand for our newly developed products all over the western world.
    6 We regret having to inform you that we cannot keep our promised date of delivery.
    7 Business transactions often begin with an enquiry (inquiry), which is made orally or in writing.
    8 This company has done/has been doing business with China for about 10 years.
    9 Modern machines are equipped with electronic surveillance/monitoring systems.
    10 We recently submitted to you our quotation for high-quality television sets.

IV 1 According to our current price list this article costs DM 50.
    2 This problem seems to be insoluble.
    3 We have not yet been able to find a solution to this problem.
    4 He has been collecting stamps for many years.
    5 This cleaning agent is innocuous.
    6 Any disadvantages should also be taken into account.
    7 His income after tax/net income is remarkably high.
    8 Please let us have your frank comments on this point.
    9 On checking our open accounts we found that our invoice dated July 22nd is overdue.
   10 He was the victim of an avalanche/a victim of circumstances.

V   1 Please send the screws by parcel post.
    2 Our staff manager has the unpleasant task of giving him (his) notice/of giving him the sack/of firing him.
    3 The shipping/forwarding agent failed to book the necessary shipping space.
    4 Under separate cover we have sent you leaflets/prospectuses/brochures on our product range/range of products.
    5 We have learnt from reliable sources that her/their company has filed a petition of bankruptcy.
    6 We would appreciate your settling our invoice at your earliest convenience/as soon as possible.
    7 All adhesive residues must be carefully removed.
    8 For reasons of safety, the machines have to be inspected every four weeks.
    9 He has been looking for an interesting job for quite a long time.
   10 This will create problems and cause inconvenience.

VI 1 In the event of malfunction, the machine will be switched off automatically.
    2 Their members came from all walks of life.
    3 The machines are operating/operate in three shifts, i.e. 24 hours a day.
    4 In the early 70s (seventies) we experienced a severe recession.
    5 Prices can be kept stable by balancing supply and demand.
    6 Finally, the proposal was agreed to by 20 votes to 2.
    7 Commercial disputes can be settled by arbitration.
    8 Every industry has its technical terms which often cannot be translated literally.
    9 Profound changes are necessary to improve this/the situation.
   10 He was deeply disappointed about loosing the match.

VII 1 She's looking for a job where she can assume responsibility.
    2 In a welfare state the unemployed get/receive unemployment benefit.
    3 We shall/will be on holiday from June 1st to June 22nd.
    4 Don't forget your important appointment in Cologne at 11 a.m.
    5 We should/would be delighted to do business with your company.
    6 A conciliation is a settlement of a commercial dispute by the parties themselves.
    7 Our sales personnel/people/staff will be pleased to advise you in more detail.
    8 We would like to ask you for a two months' extension of our credit.
    9 If your prices are reasonable, we will certainly be able to reach an agreement.
   10 Unfortunately, his business and his personal liabilities are very high.

VIII 1 Within the last two months the matter changed/has changed for the worse.
2 The Treaties of Rome were concluded in 1960.
3 Any delay in delivery will cause us great inconvenience.
4 Our stocks are completely exhausted.
5 He has made considerable progress.
6 Commitment to quality is our primary concern.
7 Payment has to be effected by irrevocable letter of credit.
8 In this case we must insist on payment in advance.
9 We exhibited our latest/most recently developed products at the Leipzig Fair.
10 One inch is 25.4 mm.

Fill in the right word:

1 subtract
2 inspection
3 attended
4 pressure
5 discontinued
6 defect
7 Promoting
8 grant
9 substantial
10 chests
11 expense
12 output
13 samples
14 break
15 programme
16 studied
17 series
18 estimated
19 obligations
20 peak
21 interference
22 borne
23 amended
24 alternative
25 target

Kapitel 2

Fill in the missing words:

1 advice (Anzeige)
2 awarded (verliehen)
3 collection (Einzugs-, Inkasso-)
4 damages (Schadensersatz)
5 execution (Ausführung)
6 issue (Problem, Streitfrage)
7 presentation (Vorlage)
8 rest (Pause)
9 settlement (Erledigung)
10 statement (...auszug)
11 terms (Bedingungen)
12 trial (Probe...)

Übersetzen Sie ins Deutsche:

1 Wir sind bereit, Ihnen in dieser Angelegenheit entgegenzukommen.
2 Bitte teilen Sie uns umgehend mit, was Sie zu tun gedenken, um die Reklamation zu regulieren.
3 Bei der Verhandlung waren keine Zuhörer zugelassen.
4 Wenn Sie bereit sind, die Ware zu behalten, werden wir Ihnen einen Nachlaß von 10 % gewähren.
5 Er sagte uns, daß die Arbeit am Fließband sehr eintönig sei.
6 Der Wechsel wurde gestern unserer Bank vorgelegt.
7 Der Aufsichtsrat kam zu dem Schluß, daß eine Diversifizierung des Lieferprogramms empfehlenswert/ratsam sei.
8 Verkaufen Sie Investitionsgüter oder Verbrauchsgüter?
9 Alle Kisten nach Übersee müssen gemäß den Anweisungen der Kunden markiert werden.
10 Wir gehen davon aus, daß Sie uns zu gegebener Zeit genauer informieren werden.
11 Die Zollbehörde verlangte eine genaue Beschreibung der von Ihnen gelieferten Artikel.
12 Der Bezogene des Wechsels war nicht in der Lage, ihn bei Fälligkeit einzulösen.
13 Es ist absolut notwendig, eine regelmäßige Kontrolle auszuüben.
14 Die Hannover Messe ist eine der bedeutendsten Messen der Welt.
15 Bitte unterbreiten Sie uns ein verbindliches Angebot über die auf beiliegender Liste spezifizierten Ersatzteile.
16 In den letzten Monaten ist der Zinssatz leicht gestieten.
17 Die Knöpfe und Tasten auf dem Bedienpult sind schwarz und rot.
18 Nachdem er 40 Jahre in dieser Branche gearbeitet hatte, trat er in den Ruhestand.
19 Wir müssen geeignete Maßnahmen ergreifen, um die Angelegenheit zur vollständigen Zufriedenheit unserer Kunden in Ordnung zu bringen.
20 Nach einer langen Diskussion entschieden sie sich dazu, das Projekt durchzuführen.
21 Das Protokoll der Sitzung enthält viele interessante Einzelheiten.
22 Sie stellten einen Antrag, dem dann stattgegeben wurde.
23 Dieser Roman ist von Simmel.
24 Ihr Altersruhegeld ist niedriger, als sie erwartet hatte.
25 Auf der diesjährigen Leipziger Messe stellten wir eine Hochleistungsmaschine zur Herstellung von Servietten aus.

26 Der Vertreter arbeitet für seinen Auftraggeber.
27 Mieten Sie sich ein Auto und besuchen Sie die schönsten Stellen unseres Landes.
29 Durch den Einsatz dieser neuen Maschine werden Sie Zeit und Geld einsparen.
29 Er spielt seit vielen Jahren Tennis und ist nun einer der erfolgreichsten Spieler unseres Vereins.
30 Der Mörder der alten Dame wurde zum Tode verurteilt.
31 Reinigen Sie die Maschine nach jeder Schicht!
32 Es waren etwa 200 junge Leute, die die verschiedenen Sprachkurse besuchten.
33 Dies ist eine solide Firma, die einen ausgezeichneten Ruf in ihrer Branche genießt.
34 Wir freuen uns, Ihnen einen Auftrag über 100 Federn Nr. 251 601 erteilen zu können.
35 Wir bedauern, Ihnen mitteilen zu müssen, daß die von Ihnen am 2. Januar bestellten Teile nicht auf Lager sind.
36 Unser Besuch an der Börse war ein großes Erlebnis.
37 Der Ersatzteilkatalog enthält die Teile, die einem erhöhten Verschleiß unterworfen sind.
38 Es gelang uns, einige neue Märkte für unsere Produkte zu finden.
39 Bitte schicken Sie uns einen Prospekt, der uns einen Überblick über Ihr Lieferprogramm gibt.
40 Eine Zeitlang war sie die beste Spielerin unserer Gruppe.

Kapitel 3

Translate into English:

1 Our shipping/forwarding agents will arrange for collection of the goods at your factory on January 21st.
2 Before entrusting him with our agency we must insist on his paying caution money.
3 Our agents are usually granted a commission of 10% on all sales within their territory.
4 We confirm that the machine you ordered is under construction.
5 They have been dealing in cars for more than 30 years and have been remarkably successful.
6 Three days ago he had a fatal accident.
7 Deliveries/consignments to certain countries must be accompanied by a certificate of origin.
8 At present business prospects are extremely good.
9 The unemployment rate in Great Britain is higher than that in Germany.
10 Within the last three months the interest rate has fallen considerably.
11 He is said to be seriously ill.
12 This company is said to be sound and solid/creditworthy.
13 The abolition of tariffs is one of the measures taken in order to further trade.
14 She tipped the waiter generously/She gave the waiter a generous tip.
15 We must insist on your treating our information as strictly confidential.
16 The merger of these two companies was a very good decision.
17 From January 1st next year, his disability pension will be increased by $2^{1}/_{2}$ percent.
18 Our design department is overburdened, and they have been working overtime for months.
19 This fellow is a real character.
20 The staff manager is the head of the personnel department.
21 We visit our customers twice a year to discuss all/any outstanding matters.
22 Any complaints must be handled with the utmost care to ensure the satisfaction of the customers concerned.

Was ist falsch?

1. concurrence (competition): Konkurrenz
   provision (commission): Provision
2. reclamation (complaint): Reklamation/Beschwerde/Mängelrüge
3. construction department (design department): Konstruktionsabteilung
4. consequently (consistently): konsequent
5. textile branch (textile trade): Textilbranche
6. prospects (leaflets, brochures): Prospekte
7. rates (instalments): Raten
8. fusion (merger): Fusion

Kapitel 4

Fill in the missing words:

1. The contract concluded between the agent and the principal was signed on August 5th.
2. We hope that both your company and ours will benefit from this cooperation.
3. Since then many new means of communication have been invented.
4. Please submit an offer stating competitive prices and terms.
5. Your consignment has given cause for complaint.
6. A complaint should be lodged at once.
7. In international trade the acknowledgement of order is often replaced by an advice of despatch.
8. Some customers of ours must apply for an import licence before importing a machine.
9. Unfortunately our order was carried out very carelessly.
10. We are in a position to deliver custom-made equipment for paper converting industries.
11. We would ask you to respond to our enquiry at your earliest convenience.
12. Marketing capital goods is different from marketing consumer goods.
13. He intends to become a foreign language correspondent.

1. It goes without saying that we will send you a credit note for the defective goods.
2. Should we suffer a loss, we shall claim damages.
3. They will further diversify their range of products.
4. You should try to contact the decision-making people of this company.
5. A detailed quotation always includes a description of the products offered.
6. I am determined to improve this unpleasant situation.
7. We very much depend on their willingness to assist us in this matter.
8. Exports to the developing countries consist mainly of capital goods.
9. Your quotation dated September 1st differs from the one you sent us three months ago.
10. Bills of exchange have three parties: the drawer, the drawee and the payee.
11. The duration of his stay is scheduled for two months.
12. The profit was distributed among the partners.
13. He works for the most successful division of this company.

1. The delay in the execution of our order has caused us great inconvenience.
2. Exports have risen to some extent.
3. For orders exceeding 1000 pieces we shall grant a quantity discount of 10%.

4 According to the latest estimates German firms have invested more than twenty thousand million in various small Asian countries.
5 The price is to be understood ex works Cologne, excluding costs for packing, freight and insurance.
6 One of the objectives of the EC is to coordinate the economic policies of the member countries.
7 They laid special emphasis on the high quality of their products.
8 At next year's Hanover Fair they will exhibit some new products.
9 These parts of the machine are particularly exposed to paper dust.
10 Payment will be effected by cheque.
11 Please return the consignment at our expense.
12 I have learnt from your advertisement in today's FAZ that you are seeking an efficient salesman.
13 We erroneously invoiced 30 units instead of the 20 units we sent you.
14 On October 1st, three new employees joined our company.
15 Our bookkeeping department made some wrong entries and it took them several days to find the mistakes.
16 It is their firm intention to expand even further.

1 There has been a decline in investments within the last three months.
2 The International Monetary Fund (IMF) was established in 1945.
3 They are anxious to introduce their articles onto new markets.
4 Your complaint is not justified.
5 Please investigate this matter.
6 They have considerable funds at their disposal.
7 They have most modern production facilities.
8 An Englishman named Rowland Hill invented the Penny Post.
9 The suspect was released after he had proved his identity.
10 I have no fault to find with him.
11 I was under the impression that something was wrong with him.
12 In business everybody is judged by their success.

1 For lubrication of the machine see the attached maintenance programme.
2 He did not obey the rules.
3 The failure of a customer of ours has caused us considerable losses.
4 Errors and omissions excepted.
5 A bill becomes a law.
6 His certificate must be legalized.
7 Merchandise is a synonym for goods.
8 The operation of this machine is very complicated and must be simplified.
9 The police officer told us how to get to the tourist information office.
10 Our new office occupies the whole of the third floor in this building.

1 Thin profit margins have forced us to reduce costs wherever possible.
2 The meeting had to be postponed.
3 They preferred tea to coffee.
4 His statement proved to be true.
5 Her boss prevented her from leaving by giving her a rise.
6 The secretary had some problems with the new text-processing system.
7 I enclose a personal data sheet with details on my education and experience as a secretary.

8 Finally he found a publisher for his novel.
9 We must make provisions for doubtful debts.
10 Production is becoming more and more automated.
11 The proprietor of this blocks of flats had the roof repaired.
12 We must obtain his permission to spend more money on our office equipment.
13 The goods were promised for delivery within a fortnight.
14 It was the same procedure as every year.
15 We wish you a happy and prosperous New Year.

1 It is safe to extend the credit of this company.
2 A cheque must be presented for payment within a reasonable time.
3 Delivery can be effected immediately after receipt of order.
4 If the quality of your articles comes up to our expectations, you may count on repeat orders.
5 The Federal Government and the "Deutsche Bundesbank" are responsible for keeping the currency stable.
6 Last year, they established a subsidiary in the United States.
7 This machine is suitable for producing paper handkerchiefs.
8 Any information you can supply will be much appreciated.
9 We should be pleased if we could resume business relations with your company.
10 Due to lack of money this project could not be realized.
11 They are not familiar with the German customs regulations.
12 Little now remains to be done.
13 This company is known for high quality standards.
14 His success is due to hard work.
15 The police questioned the suspect.
16 He is responsible for the supervision of all aspects of manufacture.
17 Summarizing, we can state that the exhibition was a great success.
18 The new airport has installed a complicated surveillance system.

1 After carefully studying your offer we have decided to place a trial order with you.
2 The goods have been paid for by bank transfer.
3 The parts are urgently required and should be delivered by the end of this month.
4 This company badly needs some good technicians.
5 The travel agency gave us some useful information about Great Britain.
6 You may rely on our treating your information as strictly confidential.
7 The theft was reported to the police.
8 He has been working in this trade for a very long time.
9 Her work permit is no longer valid.
10 A contract is concluded between companies or individuals; a treaty is concluded between states.

Translate into English:

1. They were forced to discontinue production.
2. They expressed their disapproval very clearly.
3. This letter has been written in a very impersonal and impolite manner.
4. Unfortunately it is impossible for us to accept your conditions.
5. The keen competition has discouraged them from continuing their work in this market.
6. The measures which you have taken are absolutely inadequate for improving the situation.
7. The table/chart of the recommended lubricants is still incomplete.
8. I regret having to say that he is working more and more inefficiently./Unfortunately his work is becoming/getting more and more inadequate.
9. They have insufficient means at their disposal.
10. Payment will be effected by confirmed and irrevocable letter of credit to be opened with a German bank.
11. Non-acceptance of the goods caused great inconvenience.
12. We distinguish between solicited and unsolicited offers.
13. She has been working very carelessly for some time.
14. It will be useless to follow up this matter.

Kapitel 5

Translate into English:

1. Please send us your acknowledgement of order at your earliest convenience stating the shortest possible time of delivery.
2. She would prefer to become a nurse.
3. All information will be treated as strictly confidential.
4. Have you read her/the note which she left for you?
5. It has proved advantageous for new employees to receive extensive training.
6. It is advisable to have an agent in an overseas country, because he is familiar with all (the) local regulations.
7. The United States is a relatively young nation.
8. The Government will have to discuss the question whether development aid can be increased.
9. We must insist on your granting us an allowance on the total amount of your invoice dated 21st February.
10. How do you intend to adjust/settle our complaint?
11. Delivery will be effected about the 3rd quarter of next year.
12. A bill of exchange can be discounted and prolonged.
13. She is responsible for sales promotion in this company and has an interesting job.
14. Mr Miller will be back from holiday in about one week. He will contact you immediately after his return.
15. We will pay you a visit in the week commencing March ...

Übersetzen Sie ins Deutsche:

1. Wir möchten diese Angelegenheit auf gütlichem Wege regeln und bieten Ihnen deshalb einen Nachlaß von 10% an.
2. Um Ihnen die Einführung der Produkte auf dem englischen Markt zu erleichtern, werden wir Ihnen auf den ersten Auftrag einen Rabatt von 15% gewähren.
3. Sie verfügen über die modernsten Werkzeugmaschinen.
4. Da Sie im Laufe des letzten Jahres ingesamt 12 Anzeigen geschaltet haben, gewähren wir Ihnen den in Aussicht gestellten Bonus von 5% auf alle Rechnungsbeträge.
5. Wir erinnern uns gerne der bei Ihnen in Deutschland verbrachten Zeit.
6. Wir besuchen regelmäßig die wichtigsten Ausstellungen in Deutschland und im Ausland.
7. Bitte entschuldigen Sie, daß wir es leider versäumten, für Ihre Hotelunterkunft zu sorgen.
8. Unsere tägliche Arbeit wird immer schwieriger und hektischer.
9. Die Reform der EG-Agrarpolitik ging langsam voran.
10. Prinzipiell stimmen wir dieser Vereinbarung zu; es sind lediglich noch einige kleine Änderungen zu besprechen.
11. Diese Kisten sind für Übersee bestimmt und müssen markiert werden.
12. Ein Unternehmer hat viele Risiken zu tragen.
13. Die Texte von Werbebriefen müssen besonders sorgfältig geschrieben werden.
14. Dürfen wir Sie daran erinnern, daß unsere Rechnung vom 25. Februar über £850 überfällig ist. Bitte überweisen Sie diesen Betrag auf eines unserer Konten.

Kapitel 6

Setzen Sie den oder die fehlenden Buchstaben ein:

1. Unfortunately, we cannot accept your offer.
2. I urgently need your advice.
3. Your name was given us by the German embassy in Madrid.
4. The managers always travel first class.
5. She has a strong belief in delegation.
6. Private housebuilding seems to have peaked this year.
7. Prices have been fairly stable.
8. Last year there was a slight rise in mortgage rates.
9. The principal and traditional functions of commercial banks are to accept deposits and to supply industry with circulating capital in the form of short-term loans.
10. Twelve countries have joined the EC.
11. The drawee accepts a draft by writing his name across the face of the bill.
12. The new Stock Exchange account opened in quite a depressed mood yesterday.
13. Dissolution of a partnership may also be effected by a decree of the court.
14. A corporation is a legal entity.
15. If your articles meet our requirements, we shall place a substantial order with you.
16. Delivery of the goods can be effected in about two weeks.
17. We must win back old customers who have ceased placing orders with us.
18. An offer is firm unless it contains a clause to the contrary.
19. The range of their products includes Scottish Tweeds.
20. Please, indicate length, width and height of the machine.
21. We can offer both a stationary and a portable version of this unit.

22 It helps me save a lot of time and money.
23 We are also in a position to supply more than the quantity ordered.
24 Many support the former alternative, but I personally favour the latter.
25 Before making a decision as to whether we will place an order with you, we ask to arrange for a sample to be sent to us.
26 Unless we can offer our goods at more favourable prices, we will lose customers.
27 The prices for meals are quite reasonable there.
28 She wanted to see some of the sights of London before she continued her journey to Leeds.
29 They enjoyed their ride on the bus very much.
30 When he caught sight of her, he shouted in a loud voice.
31 Big Ben is very dear to most English people.
32 I wonder whether goods are more expensive in England than in Germany.
33 The Queen regularly receives ambassadors and other diplomatic representatives.
34 The importance of the House of Lords has diminished increasingly in the course of time.
35 In Germany tennis has been playing a predominant role for some years now.
36 The ties between the Commonwealth countries have become looser and looser.
37 In his election campaigns, Kennedy pleaded for peace and equal rights for all citizens.
38 We can now advise you that the consignment was shipped by rail this morning.
39 Your cooperation in this matter would be much appreciated.
40 On the occasion of that meeting he was awarded the prize.
41 The goods have to be packed carefully to ensure safe arrival.
42 Please let us know whether gross and net weights are to be stencilled on the cases.
43 A receipt is a proof of payment.
44 We have no hesitation in granting them credit to the extent you mentioned.
45 They have done business with us for the past two years.
46 The delays in the execution of our orders are causing us great inconvenience.
47 Your information was passed on to our customers.
48 We are afraid that all this will have serious consequences for our company.
49 We shall do our utmost to meet this deadline.
50 Owing to bad weather the vessel could not sail.
51 They formally invited us for dinner.
52 All his staff were dismissed, because he closed down his business.
53 The brakes on your car must be repaired immediately.
54 As agreed upon, insurance will be covered by you.
55 All boys and girls of the class passed the examination, except him.
56 We believe you will never find a better one.
57 We build machines and equipment for the chocolate and confectionery industry.
58 This envelope machine can be equipped with a device for producing pockets.
59 For the past twenty years I have been employed by Smithe and Horton.
60 They seek to raise their standard of living.
61 He delivered a most interesting speech.
62 Please lay the book on my desk. The book lies on my desk.

Kapitel 8:

Fill in the missing prepositions:

1. Three years ago, we entered into negotiations with this supplier, but we have not yet come to terms.
2. I cannot agree to your suggestion to deliver the goods one month later, because these spare parts are urgently needed.
3. They applied for the import licence, but so far it has not yet been granted by the authorities.
4. They have been dealing with this matter for quite a long time.
5. We have drawn on you for the amount of our invoice dated December 1st.
6. He will have lunch at a restaurant, because it would take him too long to come home.
7. The above mentioned order covers 10 different articles.
8. Acts of God are beyond our control.
9. The letter of recommendation was written by his secretary.
10. Please forward the consignment by airfreight.
11. Apart from two days at Christmas, Mr Steed has not had a day off for ten months.
12. You will have all amenities at your disposal.
13. Be careful on the road!
14. He stayed with his parents for three hours.
15. First they had a look at Buckingham Palace.
16. He is not as good at cricket as his brother.
17. For an order of 100 units and more we are prepared to grant you a quantity discount of 15%.
18. The goods you have ordered will be delivered subject to our usual terms and conditions.
19. We hope that this order will be executed by the end of this month.
20. Essen and its surroundings are rich in coal.
21. Charles is a student at the University of Oxford.
22. Most parents are proud of their children.
23. Electric light came into use towards the end of the 19th century.
24. Let us have a look behind the scenes.
25. I know her only by name.
26. When does the next train leave for Cologne?
27. In my opinion your parents are wrong.
28. If the articles meet with our customers' approval, you may count on substantial orders from us.
29. Please look into the matter and let us have your comments at your earliest convenience.
30. We are looking forward to your reply with great interest.
31. The goods have been delivered except for item 0231 which is out of stock.
32. He is not interested in his father's business.
33. The poor old lady had to live on very little money.
34. Our present management is quite different from what it was.
35. Over the past ten years our working conditions and our wages have improved considerably.
36. I am at a loss how to assist you in this matter.
37. My principal is away on business; he will not be back until Monday.
38. The articles will be paid for by cheque.
39. She is eagerly waiting for the doctor who has been operating on her husband for three hours now.
40. Increase in production is our most important objective for the coming year.
41. We are looking for an agent who has experience in the North American market.

42 Please find enclosed our invoice amounting to £998.
43 We refer to your recent inquiry.
44 They came across many difficulties which they did not know how to solve.
45 He used to live above his means.
46 We regret having to inform you that a decision has been made in favour of your competitors.

Notizen

Notizen

Notizen